Self Publishing Success

A HANDBOOK FOR NEW WRITERS

Mary Rosenblum

Promontory Press

Promontory Press
1628 Dean Park Road
North Saanich, BC V8L 4Y7
http://www.promontorypress.com/

Book Layout ©2013 BookDesignTemplates.com

Self Publishing Success/ Mary Rosenblum. —1st ed.
ISBN 978-1-927559-22-2

Contents

For Nate and Jake

Many thanks to authors Alexis Glynn Latner and Dale Ivan Smith for their invaluable input on this project.

CHAPTER 1

Welcome to Indie

Hello and welcome to the brave new world of Indie! That's independent publishing, also known as self-publishing. Not so long ago, it used to be called vanity publishing and all the 'real' authors curled their lips. Meant you were a loser. You were so bad, you had to pay to get published. Wow, have things changed in the last five years! Now, you have well established New York authors jumping ship to publish their next books themselves, and boasting about how they are making more money and selling more books that way than they ever did with the New York houses. The media went wild with hot stories about this or that unknown writer who stuck their new book up on Amazon.com and sold a million copies. Our local paper made it sound as if all you needed to do was slap that ebook up on a site and sit back to rake in the cash as an instant best seller. Guaranteed!

Well, a whole lot of people discovered that a year later, with ten of their self-published books sold, that this wasn't actually the case. Then the wail went up that the 'epublishing revolution was over' and self-publishing was – once more – a loser's path.

Oh, *please.*

Independent publishing is a very valid path to your publishing goal, whether that goal is simply to get your beloved book or personal memoir in front of readers, or to make a living as a self-supporting career writer. You face the same issues as the New York published writers of my time, although the way the books you write earn you money is different for each path. You will probably not become a blockbuster best seller. We all hope for that lovely brass ring when we get onto this merry-go-round, but only a very few authors, whether New York published or Indie published, actually achieve those breathtaking million-sales numbers. But, as what New York used to call a 'mid-list author', that is, an author who makes steady sales and has a slowly building fan base, but is not a best-seller and household word, you can build a career that will allow you to write full time and live comfortably. No, it will not be handed to you on a silver platter, folks. It will be a day job. The image of the writer who spends fifteen minutes in his mahogany paneled study writing in his bathrobe, before changing into his yachting togs and heading out to luncheon at the club has always been a complete myth. It's a pretty one, but it's still a myth. I supported myself and my two sons on my writing and it was a 40 plus hour a week day job. I was mid-list.

But it was the day job of my dreams!

So, who am I? I'm Mary Rosenblum, the literary midwife. I wrote SF as Mary Rosenblum and mystery as Mary Freeman full time for more than two decades. And I taught writing. As part of teaching, I started helping my students get published. I got sick of the slick scam 'publishers' and 'agents' who preyed on their dreams, raked in lots of money in 'fees', and then betrayed them, so I started making sure that my students got published by legitimate publishers who earned money from the book's sales, rather than from those fees the scammers convinced their victims to pay. I welcomed the publishing revolution as ebooks burst on the scene and authors discovered that yes, you could sell just as many books on Amazon.com if you published yourself as you could if you were published by a New York publisher. Readers did not care about the publisher, they cared about the book!

Anyone could publish now, and everyone did. The internet book-selling sites were inundated with self-published books of all levels of quality. And the scammers started raking it in. Open up your browser, visit one writing-related website and suddenly you find a host of ads on your screen. Publish with us! Publish for 500$! Become a Best Seller Overnight! they scream. This brave new world of publishing is infested with sharks, folks. And once again, I found myself rescuing students from fabulous pitch letters sent by charming 'publishers' who would make your book a best seller in a heartbeat. No problem! *Just pay for our 'quality' editing service, a really nice cover, oh, and our promotional package. For a hefty price. That 500$ we quoted you? Oh, that was just the basic plan, but you need much much more! If you want to succeed...* Of course you got no apology for the ten books that sold in the first year. *Oh well, I guess readers didn't like what you wrote.*

It's too expensive to self-publish, my students whined over and over.

Say what? I took a good look at what was going, got mad, and decided it was time for some honesty in this game.

That's when I started The New Writers Interface and became a literary midwife.

I'm a reader. I love the opportunities that this new wild world of publishing has opened up for me. No longer are my choices limited by the decisions of the New York publishers' marketing department. I want those good books to read and I want those new books to be as good as the author can possibly make them. So I started helping clients produce the best book they could, get it published well with a legitimate, quality publisher, and learn how to promote it effectively, so that they didn't get lost in the sea of books out there and find themselves with ten books sold after the first year.

It's an ongoing process, since the publishing world changes every day, at the speed of the internet. I spend a lot of time keeping an eye on what is working for Indie authors and what is not working, as well as the changes in the publishing trends. Subscribe to my *Literary Midwife Newsletter* for updates and news to keep you up on what is going on. This book will give you an overview of what it takes to succeed with your book and how to make it happen for you.

Welcome to Indie! It's a brave new world out there!

Mary Rosenblum

The Literary Midwife

www.newwritersinterface.com

CHAPTER 2

Publishing Yourself Today

Let's start out with a little history here. You'll understand today's publishing world better if you understand how we got here. It'll all make more sense!

Once upon a time, back before I started publishing in the eighties, there were many New York publishers, mostly small, some large. And the editors and the publishers at those houses mostly loved books and weren't just in it for the bottom line, although yeah, they had to keep the lights on. They had their bread-and-butter publishing jobs; text books, maybe even brochures, stuff that sold reliably and paid the electric bill and the authors and made a profit. But those publishers and editors were book people and they wanted to bring really good books to their readers. Why? Because they loved really good books.

Not all those early books they published made a profit at first, even though many became classics later on. Then, as now, it was a gamble. Would readers like this book or really love it? But there was enough profit in the steady bread-and-butter sales to carry these authors who maybe didn't pay out, or make back the cost of publishing and shipping the books to bookstores. They might lose money on their first couple of books, but eventually built a respectable reader-ship and became big sellers. It takes time to build a reader-ship, when you're a brand new author. Before the internet and Facebook, it took longer for readers to spread the word that this book was great.

Not every book had to be a best seller. The publishing houses stood, not only on a foundation of bread-and-butter books, but also what came to be known as the mid-list. These were books that earned the company profits over the cost of production, but not stunning profits. They weren't the stars, but they were steady earners.

Things began to change. The cost of book production rose with the rising costs of paper and labor. The increasing options on television started to take a bite out of the paper-back market. As a kid growing up in a blue-collar area of Pittsburgh, I used to see steel-workers waiting at the bus stops with their lunch boxes at their sides, a bodice-ripper mystery, pulp science fiction, or thriller in their hands. You've seen the old pulp covers, haven't you? Lots of bare female skin. You gotta love those Warrior Women of Mars gals. Me, I wouldn't want to swing a broadsword in a chain-mail biki-ni…but I digress. The leisure time that got spent on those pulp-fiction thrillers now started going into the TV serials. And book sales started to drop.

The publishing houses, faced with rising production costs and declining sales, started to merge. This has been and still is a continuing trend. As recently as 2012, we saw the Big Six remaining New York, or legacy publishers contract to become the Big Four. With every merger, the companies shed authors. You may have been selling your crime novels to your regular publisher, but now, in the new, merged house, if your sales numbers weren't as good as the authors that the acquiring publishing house regularly bought from, or your editor had been let go, your next novel might well get rejected. Now, you had to find a new publishing home. Already, it was getting tougher for new authors to break into the business.

The tax structure changed. The government now began to tax book inventories. Those big warehouses full of mid-list books waiting to ship to bookstores became a financial liability. Suddenly, the small, steady earnings of the mid-list author no longer covered the cost of storing those books and counting them as assets on Tax Day. The profit margins were shrinking for these big companies as our leisure time became more and more divided. Movie rentals and then, Facebook, started taking a bigger and bigger share. Book sales kept dropping, book prices inched up, and the companies started paying much more attention to how much money a book made *right now*. No longer were they willing to wait while an author built a fan base and perhaps became that best-selling author they so desperately needed.

When I started publishing, in the late eighties, authors got three to four books to 'prove' themselves at most houses. If sales were increasing, if the author was winning awards, getting rave reviews in the big review magazines like *Kirkus, New York Times Review of Books,* and *Library Journal,* they'd keep you on. If your sales were pretty flat, or your books didn't 'earn out' and pay back the advance against royalties that is a perk of the New York author, you were gone. You'd have to find another publisher to sell to.

This situation kept getting worse, and now the electronic age was upon us. Distributors and bookstores merged their data-bases, so that sales of your book in every store were at the fingertips of the buyers and there was no way to hide poor sales. Brick and mortar bookstores weren't making much money either. They couldn't afford to keep your book on the shelf if it didn't earn a chunk of the rent, so if your first novel had really bad sales, the buyers would order only the number of copies of Book Two that had sold for Book One.

And the bookstores stopped reordering.

That meant you had to have great sales with book one if you wanted to have good sales with the next book. The only way around this was to change your name and become a 'new' author. Quite a few writer friends of mine are on their third or even fourth incarnation with the same publisher, trying for that jumpstart in the system. Alas, it makes it difficult for the fan who loved Book One to find Book Two. That fan is looking for a book by the same author and that author now has a new name. Makes it tough for the author to get ahead.

And that brings us to the Brass Ring Factor of today's legacy publishing world.

Today's ideal paradigm in the legacy publishing world is the First Book Best Seller. That's what they're after. They want the *Twilight* or the *Harry Potter* that sells a million books right out of the gate. More than one publishing insider has told me that if a publishing house does not get one of these block-buster authors in a year, they lose money. If that's true, it's a pretty fragile system there and it may explain our recent contraction from Big Six to Big Four.

But that is now what the editor is looking for when you submit a novel to the legacy publishers. It's all about the market and what the marketing department thinks is the Next Hot Thing. That's what the agents are looking for, too. That Next Hot Thing that the marketing people have decided on. It's no longer about publishing a good book. It's about publishing a book that sells a million or three copies immediately.

Would we have Hemingway or Hillerman's mysteries if they had started publishing today? Navajo cops? *Forget it! It's all about vampires this year! Fishing? Nobody wants to read a book about some old guy sitting in a boat all day...*

The mid-list is pretty much gone. It still exists in a very few small legacy houses that persist today. Daw is one of those houses. But for the most part, you're going to get one chance on this merry –go-round to snag that brass ring and head toward best-seller status. There's also a new and to me, disturbing trend. A lot of new authors are celebrities from another arena; sports stars, or TV personalities. If you are a popular TV weatherman with a mystery, or an NBA basketball star, hey, your thriller may not be as good as this one by Ms. New Author, but a whole lot of people are going to buy it, just because Mr. Weatherman or the NBA player wrote it.

Marketability over quality seems to bo today's trend In the legacy world.

It also, alas, makes it very difficult for the new author with no celebrity status and no pre-existing fan base to get serious attention from the legacy publishers. Yes, if your book is lucky enough to fit the marketing department's 'hot new trend' then you may well get picked up. A suspense writer I know was picked up because the publisher hoped he'd become the 'next Grisham'. If you don't fit the increasingly narrow market-niches of the legacy world, however, then you're out of luck.

And that, as a reader, makes me very sad. I want books that are new, fresh, that surprise me, challenge me. I don't want another Harry Potter or Grisham. And it's less and less likely that I'll find that surprise or challenge coming out of New York.

Enter Amazon.com and the birth of Independent Publishing. Hang onto your hats, we're in for a wild ride!

The Brave New World

Okay, let me establish one thing right here. I'm going to throw Amazon.com's name around a lot here. Right now, a number of writers, readers, and not a few organizations such as Author's Guild, of which I am a member, see Amazon.com as a new Evil Empire gobbling up the online publishing world. I am far less than thrilled with everything they do, and with increasing market share and market power comes an increasing opportunity to gain that strangle-hold on publishing that the legacy gate-keepers once enjoyed. I hope we can keep that from happening, and I sure plan to do my part to keep this an open playing field. But there is no denying that Amazon.com and their marketing model propelled us into this new age of publishing. I am not endorsing the Amazon.com of today or its actions, but they do deserve credit for their role in what we have now. Hey, Amazon, if you read this? Behave yourselves, huh? Stay ethical. I know that's not easy for the type of big company you have become, but let's keep this a publishing world that benefits readers first, eh? You'll still make money!

We're going to start with the internet, since Amazon.com couldn't exist without it. While Facebook, online games, and email ate big holes in leisure reading time, they also gave us the ability to share our personal news with not just the folk in the office or our buddies, but with friends, acquaintances, relatives, and the general public. If you loved that book you just read, you raved about it on Facebook and some of your Facebook Friends read it, liked it, and raved about it on their Facebook pages. Viral marketing was born and the numbers could grow much much faster now than they ever had through the water-cooler grapevine or the after-church coffee hour.

What Amazon.com did was to begin to change the way readers bought their next new read. It used to be that most everybody walked into their local bookstore. Perhaps most came looking for the new book from a familiar author or the title that a friend had recommended, but then they browsed the New Release shelf. That's where the books published by the New York legacy publishers were displayed. No, you didn't find many, if any, books from small press publishers there. The bookstore owner could get the legacy books on consignment. If the book didn't sell, they returned the unsold hardcovers to the publisher to be remaindered, and stripped the covers from the paperbacks to send those covers in for a refund. Small press publishers couldn't afford to do that. They had to sell those books to the bookstore owner outright. If that book didn't sell, it took up valuable space and made the owner no money. Bottom line? Bookstores sold legacy published books pretty much exclusively.

Amazon.com changed all this. Now you could find a title on Amazon.com and often, it was cheaper than the copy in the brick-and-mortar bookstore. And, a nice list of 'customers who bought this also bought...' suggestions popped right up on the page for you. Not all these books were legacy published books. In fact, many many were not. Alas, the downside of this was that it pulled the economic rug out from under the feet of many small independent bookstores. These stores were operated by people who loved books and often ran them while holding a day job that paid the real money they needed to live on. Many of them were not able to find a way to stay in business as Amazon.com offered the same books for less money. That is a very unfortunate side-effect of this change and some wonderful bookstores went under.

Suddenly, however, small press published and self-published books, got equal shelf space with the legacy books – at least on Amazon.com's virtual store shelves.

This, folks, was the beginning of the revolution.

But the Indie explosion didn't happen right off the bat. There was a lot of prejudice against self-published books. When legacy publishers were the only game in town, along with a few small press houses who sold to independent bookstores, authors who had to pay to publish their books were tagged as 'losers'. Their books must be so poor that no commercial publisher would touch them! And often, alas, that was the case. You did have some niche titles whose readership was too small to interest the legacy publishers (think real estate agents), but where an author could market directly to that narrow market and make a reasonable return from that self-published book. But that was the exception. Self-publishing was sneeringly referred to as 'vanity publishing' and vanity-press books were specifically excluded from awards. Well known reviewers rarely if ever reviewed them.

That wall began to crack as some mid-list authors who had lost their places with the contracting legacy publishers, but already had a fan base, started publishing their next books themselves. Publishing technology had changed. Print on Demand technology mean that a publishers could set up and print a relatively small number of copies for a reasonable per-book production cost, and with some effort, the author could pay for distribution through one of the book distribution companies. (*Ingrams* and *Baker and Taylor* are the two Big Distribution Companies, today). That book still wouldn't make it into the chain bookstores unless the author pitched it successfully to the buyer for a specific store, but it would be available on Amazon.com, the author's website, and any independent bookstores that agreed to stock it. And some of those authors were making reasonable sales. Most legacy authors, however, still turned up their noses at it as 'vanity press'. Not many authors walked around at writers conferences boasting about their self-published books, and most created a publisher name to go on the cover, so that readers did not realize that the book had been published by the author.

Slowly, however, the sales of self-published books began to increase online. It still worked best for authors who had brought their own fan base to the self-publishing world with them. As a new writer, it was a tough row to hoe. Most people still learned of new books from the New Release shelf in the brick and mortar bookstore, from a friend's recommendation, a review, or an interview with the author. The reviews and interviews were tough to get, back in the days of 'vanity press'.

Come The e-Revolution

Enter the ebook. At first it evoked a lot of sneering. *Who wants an e-reader? You gonna take it into the bathtub? Onto the hammock under the maple? Who wants to read onscreen? Paper books will never die!* Well, I sure agree with that, but they may well end up the niche market to the mainstream ebook! At first, the e-readers were kind of clunky, hard to read, and not very popular. At the same time, the music scene was changing radically and people were downloading their next song from iTunes, rather than buying that expensive CD, never mind the vanishing vinyl. We need an iPod for the ebook, people said.

Amazon.com, whose marketing people are on things, came out with the Kindle.

Essentially they gave it away. It wasn't as cheap as a single book, but considering that you could download a library onto it and at a fraction of the cost of buying those same books as paperbacks, it found an immediate following, in spite of the scoffing. Romance readers, many of whom go through several books in a week, embraced the platform first. I had clients who were publishing in both ebook and paper with small press romance publishers long before I saw the same interest in the other genres. Amazingly enough, older folk embraced it as well. "I have ten books right here," a veterinarian friend in his seventies exulted, waving his Kindle at me. "And I can make the print larger!" This was the first Kindle that Amazon.com released, and when I heard

Jack's enthusiasm, I figured the Kindle and other e-readers to come were here to stay.

Amazon.com's marketing cleverness went one step farther. Not only could you buy the Kindle cheap and buy ebooks to load on it that cost a whole lot less than the print version, but they now started a self-publishing service for that Kindle.

Aspiring authors could upload their own books and publish them for the Kindle.

The dam burst.

And it was a very very smart move on Amazon.com's part. If you upload your beloved novel as an ebook, your family and friends all have to have Kindles in order to read it, right? Clever, clever, Amazon.com! They were smart enough, too, to make it easy for even the technology-challenged to upload that Word file directly to ebook status. Alas, the consequences of this type of instant gratification were pretty woeful in most cases, and the perception that self-published ebooks were garbage was pretty easy to justify at first.

Self-publishing was still for losers and ebooks were uploaded by illiterates who didn't bother to spell-check their manuscripts first, never mind learn how to write well or, heaven forbid, format the page properly! You could find plenty of examples to justify those statements, believe me. However, that did not stop Amazon.com and now Barnes and Noble and Sony from following Amazon.com's model, giving us the Nook and Sony e-reader. Apple was a bit slower to get onboard, perhaps because music was such a huge platform on iTunes. Late to the game, they have not caught up as of today, but give them time. The iPad mini may trump the e-reader yet, and more and more people are reading on their smart-phones – often an iPhone.

Then, a few authors with strong fan bases decided that their royalties from the legacy publishers were pretty paltry compared to what you could earn on your own with an ebook and decided to give the self-publishing thing a try. Once upon a time, New York didn't include electronic rights in their contracts and if they did, your agent could negotiate them back for you. (That's no longer the case). So these authors were able to publish their 'back list' of books that had originally been published by New York companies, as ebooks.

The first stories of million-book sales on Amazon.com broke in the papers and Indie Mania was born! This story became the darling of the media and the news stories were eye-rollers, making it sound as if every single title uploaded as an ebook turned into an instant best-seller. The truth was, big-number sellers, such as John Scalzi, already had a solid fan base when they started their ebook publishing careers. Scalzi was not a brand new, no name-recognition, new author. And he is a darn good writer, too.

I remember getting a call from my eighty year old neighbor as this storm was breaking, exhorting me to quit my student and client work, upload my backlist of mystery and SF books, and sit back to become a millionaire. Well, yeah, I did need to get those darn books uploaded, I was the cobbler's child for sure, shoeless as I worked on client books, but I shook my head. I knew better. I'd watched students and clients publish since before all this started to change and the hype was just that – hype. The media grabbed a few high-profile cases and made some sweeping generalizations without bothering to do any real homework. The writing and publishing bloggers who *did* know what was going on mostly joined me in the eye-rolling, but I have to say, it did stimulate a lot of ebook interest, so hey, it wasn't a bad thing.

We're now up to today and the well established presence of the online bookstores, ebooks, and Indie publishing. We have a big new playing field, and you have the ability to start out as a brand new author whose name nobody knows, and find your fans. But it's not a matter of merely uploading that book as an ebook or to a POD publishing platform and waiting for the cash to roll in. Not quite!

Long Tail Versus Short Wag

Let's look first at how book sales look today, for the Indie publisher, as compared to how they looked yesterday, when I was a mid-list legacy author.

In the legacy model, your book was published, ads went out to the appropriate magazines in your genre, and reviews showed up in the major review markets; *New York Times Review of Books, Kirkus, Library Journal,* and some of the major metropolitan newspapers. The bookstores shelved your book, hopefully, on the New Release shelf, and readers browsing for that next good thriller, or mystery, or self-help, or what have you, got a chance to eyeball your marketing-department-blessed cover and read the catchy blurb on the back. (Good blurb copy is an art and people who do it well get paid accordingly in New York. Book jacket blurbs from legacy-published books are a great place to learn how to do it well).

These first months of publication were the best time for authors to arrange readings at their local bookstores or libraries, hand out bookmarks or trinkets at conferences, and generally do what they could to promote their work. These first six months to a year were also the critical time period for book sales. These numbers, good or bad, determined your future with that book and maybe that publisher. You were most likely going to make your peak sales as the 'new book' in this first year. Each bookstore only stocked so many copies on its shelves. Once they were gone, few bookstores in the big chains were willing to reorder unless they had lots of demands. If they did not sell all their copies, they would order that many fewer copies of your next book, and your chances of selling more copies with Book Two diminished significantly. So those first sales were critical and authors chewed their nails, hoping for a rapid increase in sales, indicating an enthusiastic and growing fan base.

For most authors, that first year was the high water mark of their sales for that book. Some did go on to grow quickly and steadily in popularity, and if their sales numbers exceeded the 'benchmark' of the house they were publishing with, they could continue to sell books there, and would hopefully build to a level of sales that guaranteed them a home. But the majority of first time authors saw those numbers fall beneath the house benchmark and decrease after that initial advertising and review push ended. Remember that New York publishers incur a lot of expensive overhead when they publish books, and they expect a 'successful' book to pay for itself, the books that do not cover their production costs, and earn money for the publishing house as well. The benchmark sales numbers for the New York publishers are very very high. You're going to need to sell over 50,000 copies in a year in order to impress anybody.

If the numbers weren't above the house benchmark, If you were not being strongly supported by the publisher as a potential best-seller author, your numbers generally continued to drop and when you got below a certain level, perhaps a year or two or three down the road, or when the publishing house decided they were not going to continue to publish your books, your book went Out of Print, or OP. It was no longer available new, even if fans requested it from the bookstore. You could also get your rights back. Now, that has changed significantly today, and we'll talk about that later on, when I get to the section on publishing, rights, and what to beware of in contracts, but let's not put the cart ahead of the horse here.

Overall, a legacy author's sales peaked early and diminished steadily, until the book was only available on the used book market. You don't earn any royalties from a used book, and that could be a serious problem if the early books in a series were only available on the used market, while later books were still selling in the bookstores. Yes, that did happen. Quite often. The downside was that readers who read your recent book and loved it might buy all your earlier books, but they were second-hand, and you didn't earn a dime. So your sales of new books reflected a slowly growing increase, while the overall sales of books you had written might be taking off, building some serious numbers. Not only did you not earn a dime for those second-hand sales but the publisher was oblivious to them. So your official sales numbers looked poor. It was not a good situation for the mid-list author who was once able to earn a sustainable income when his or her entire backlist was still available to sell new and thus, to earn royalties for the author and income for the publisher.

Call this the 'short wag' effect. Most legacy authors make most of their sales early and then the sales-curve goes pretty flat, unless you're a brass-ring winner and soar to bestseller status.

Why The Long Tail?

Enter the Indie author. Our author publishes his or her first book and starts working a well-thought-out promotional platform. Let's face it, there's a sea of readers out there, and your book is a drop of water in that sea. Sales numbers for the first few months to a year can be pretty awful, once all your family, friends, and blog-fans buy their copies. That author pays the rent with the day job and keeps writing. The second book goes up for sale. Then the third. Our author is a good writer, the books are professional in quality, both in terms of reader engagement and production, and word starts getting around. Book Two is more polished, the author is hitting his/her stride and the sales are better. You're not paying the rent yet, far from it, but more people like the book.

And they go buy Book One.

This is the critical diversion from the legacy paradigm. It's very possible that if that author had published through New York, that Book One would already be OP. Unavailable. But it *is* available. So they buy it, and because it is new, the author gets the royalty. (And your per-book earnings as an Indie author is quite a bit higher than what the legacy publishers will give you).

Book Three is published and our author is working on Book Four. Now, loyal readers buy the new book and readers who are new to this author and his/her books buy this book and the two previous books. For each new happy fan, the author is likely to sell three books, not one. And as the number of books published by this author grows, so do the numbers. Readers who love an author's work tend to buy and read everything that author publishes.

And none of those books go out of print.

So here, we have the exact opposite of the legacy sales curve. At first, the sales are woeful, you'll be lucky to pay for a Big Mac and fries with what you make on your first book in an early month. But if you write books that engage readers, books they enjoy and share with their friends, if you keep publishing more books, your numbers will build and so will your income. The peak sales will come down the road rather than in the first months, but they can continue forever, as long as your fans are happy with what you write and you keep writing.

Too many new self-publishing authors expect the big numbers right away and feel that their books have failed if they don't sell tens of thousands of copies in the first year. Alas, all that media-hype about million copy sales didn't help that mindset much. So the discouraged author stops blogging and slinks off with tail between legs to write a whiny article for *Salon* about the end of Indie and how it's still for losers and New York is really the Only Way To Go.

Oh, *please.*

If you don't learn how to play this new game, you aren't going to play it well.

And that's why you're reading this book. Right?

You need to understand how the game is played before you can achieve your goals in this brave new publishing world. So those of you who think that you've failed if you don't meet that media-set Million Copy Sales benchmark? Get over it! Most likely it ain't gonna happen and you know what? It doesn't matter unless authoring a Best Seller is your only writing goal. And if that's the case, good luck. Myself, I'd probably invest in lottery tickets.

In Indie, success is measured by career, not by the sales of one individual book.

Keep that in mind.

It's a very nice response when someone raises their eyebrows at the woeful income you earned from that first book in the first months that it was available. A nice response is '*Just you wait!*'.

CHAPTER 3

Is Indie Right For You?

I steer quite a few clients to small press publishers or to an agent, if that client has a book that fits the current narrow market-niches of the legacy publishers. Those clients will most likely not succeed on their own, for one or more of several reasons. Independent publishing, doing the whole job yourself and reaping all the profits, is not going to work for everyone. Many new authors have found this out the hard way, after slapping that book up onto the internet and then facing dismal sales and a dawning realization that this is not how they want to proceed with publishing.

The problem is that it is so tempting to click on one of those 'publish your book right now' ads that pop up on your browser, no matter how good your pop-up controls are. It all seems so easy: Put it out there! Watch it turn into a best seller overnight! The ad copy for those companies is top-notch, platinum quality, speaking directly to every author's secret hopes and dreams and boy, are they raking in the cash! Too bad I'm ethical. I could be making a fortune. Darn ethics. They sure get in the way of financial success some-times. Unfortunately, quite a few businesses do not have a similar problem. They promise that Everything is Taken Care Of For You. Just click on the Pay Now button... . Oh, we'll talk in detail about what to beware of, a little later in this book, don't worry.

Bottom line is that it's very easy to spend a bunch of cash to pursue that golden dream of the self-published best-seller, only to end up with a book on Amazon.com that sells very few copies and leaves you with a lingering sense of failure. Even if you do Indie right, it may still not be the right path for you or your book.

How do you decide? Let's start with the basics. What do you want from your publishing venture here? What defines success for you?

Okay, we all want the Blockbuster Best Seller. I hoped for that with every book I published, for sure! Didn't happen, but that didn't mean that I didn't believe the next book might not snag me that brass ring! And they were good books. Lots of fans loved them and bought more of my work. We have to believe in that best seller, don't we? We're spending all this time isolated in front of a computer screen because we believe in what we're writing. We believe that Lots Of People Will Love It. And they will, if you do a good job of writing. Maybe not millions, but lots!

As I said earlier, if your only definition of success is that blockbuster, million-copy best-seller, you are setting yourself up for failure. Sure, it could happen, but you could win the lottery, too. Or get struck by lightning. Not many authors actually make those big sales numbers. Far fewer than you think.

So, what else, besides a best-seller, will make you feel that you have succeeded? Do you simply want to get a book in print, know that readers were moved by it, the way you were moved by books that you read? Is this another item to cross off your bucket-list? Publish a book? Do you simply want to get that memoir about Mom's life journey from Ireland to Duluth published, to honor her memory? Do you want the grandkids to understand one day where the family came from and who their ancestors were? Do you want to eventually quit your day job and pay the rent while eating better than Ramen? These are all valid goals, but they will take you down different paths.

I Just Want To See My Book In Print. Period.

That's a perfectly fine goal! What's wrong with that? I guarantee you that you can succeed with this one!

I have quite a few clients who just want to publish that book they have spent so many months or years creating. They want to hold it in their hands. They want to casually mention at that next dinner party, 'oh yes, the book is up on Amazon.com now.' One of my clients has written her memoir to hand out at her funeral – an invitation-only party she plans to throw before she passes on. (Great idea, in my opinion, why miss a good party just because you're dead?). It's a fun memoir. It's likely the only book she'll ever publish and she really doesn't care if nobody else buys it, although hey, if it snagged that magical brass ring of best-sellerdom she'd be thrilled! This book will probably sell some copies online, and may even sell a fair number if she picks up a sort of cult following. As I said, it's a fun read! But her purpose is not to have a career. The income from one book will probably never be enough to pay her bills even if fans discover her, and that is not her goal.

This is an author who needs the services of a quality subsidy publisher – a publisher who will take her money and do the work for her to get the book into print. She will pay that publisher the costs of set up and production for a well-printed book. With today's Print on Demand technology, she can order a very small number of copies to hand out at her funeral party. Or she can pay someone to format the book for her and publish it through Lulu Publishing or Create Space so that it goes up on Amazon.com. She can simply purchase the number of copies that she needs and it will be available to readers, too. She has absolutely no desire to learn page design, format the book for print, come up with a cover, and upload the book herself. She has no desire to do any promotion whatsoever. She has better things to do, thank you, like plan that funeral party.

Another client of mine published a stunningly beautiful tribute to her mother for the huge family gathering that was planned to celebrate her 85th birthday. The large-format book was filled with family photos, both in black and white and color, and was beautifully laid out. It was an expensive book to produce, printed by a subsidy press for a set up fee and a cost-per-copy contract. It was not a book that would interest many people outside the extended family and it was not intended to be a best-seller. It was not even made available for sale to the public beyond the publisher's website. It suited that author's needs perfectly.

It can be expensive to pay someone to do the technical work for you, if you plan to publish your books independently. It takes time and online effort to connect with potential readers if you're a new author, and effective self-promotion requires a regular time commitment. If you're a tech-phobe or you simply live a very very busy life and have no time to spare, small press publishers are probably your best option. The expanding marketplace today includes a growing number of small press publishers who are quite legitimate. That is, they plan on making their income from sales of your book rather than the fees they charge to the author, so they are selective about the quality of the books they publish. They are creating a pool of readers who will come to the publisher's catalogue for their next read, the way that readers visit the New Release shelf in the brick and mortar bookstores. (This is a very important distinction since many self-described small-press publishers have no interest in actually making their profits from the sales of your books. More on that later). If regular self-promotion is not something you feel you are up for, that small-press option is going to work better for you than merely slapping your book up online and hoping people will notice it. They mostly won't. The small-press publishers at least introduce your book to that pool of readers they're building.

Before you give into that urge to publish your book right now, this second, take the time to think it through. Are you willing to learn how to upload and publish your book yourself? Are you willing to pay someone to do this for you? Are you willing to take the time to promote the book yourself, so that it sells more than ten copies in a year? Is it important to earn the money that you spend on fees-for-service back? Or do you simply want that book to be available for the funeral, the birthday party, the wedding, the dinner party conversation, the family library?

Pay For It And Get It Done

If you simply want a well-published book and are willing to pay to see that book you've worked on so hard available in print or as an ebook, then shop for a subsidy publisher or an ebook formatter who will give you the best service for your money. The subsidy publisher will format and print the book for you and they can make it available to the public on their website or Amazon.com if you choose. Be a savvy consumer here! Ask questions! Compare fees! Make a list of what you want and make sure you know what they will charge for each item on your list. Be specific! You want copy editing, page design, a cover, and you want to be able to proof read the final copy and approve that page design and cover. Get that quote in writing! Will it cost extra to get an ISBN number or put the book up on Amazon.com? Make a list of questions and present it to each publisher, then compare answers from several before you decide who gets your hard-earned money.

If publishers offer you extra options or services, ask yourself if you really need them before you say yes. It is the publisher's job to sell you things, it is your job to buy only what you really want and need and to get the best quality for your dollars. Pretend you are entering a used car lot. That's the mindset you need to have. Ask *why*. Ask it a lot. If offers seem too good to be true, they are. Shop around. If you have to make up your mind 'right now' for this 'very special offer', say thank you, good-bye, and go elsewhere. It's a used car lot, remember? If you don't look under the hood and kick the tires, you're gonna be sorry!

Make sure you can proof-read the book before it is published and expect any corrections you make to be implemented before the book is published. Find out if there's an extra fee for that. There should not be, but often there is. If you're printing the book, purchase other books published by this company and take a look at the quality of the cover, the paper used inside, and how well the book is bound. Hold it. Throw it in the back of the car and leave it there for a week. Kick it around some. How does it look now? Battered is okay, destroyed is not okay. It can be pretty upsetting to pay a 'bargain rate' publisher, only to open the box with your newly-published books in it and have the pages fall from the poorly-glued cover, or discover that ten pages are missing, right from the climax of the murder mystery! Suddenly that 'bargain rate' isn't such a bargain, is it? You think that can't happen, huh? It has. One author, who has rather impressive sales numbers, received a shipment of her newly-published book right before a critical seminar, only to discover that the poor-quality paper used in the production of the book allowed the pages and cover to curl badly in a humid environment. The book looked unprofessional and reflected poorly on the content of what is an excellent book.

Remember that ad copy is just that; ad copy. Of course the publisher promises you the earth and the sky for a pittance. Remember what the business of the seller is? Uh huh. They want you to buy what they're selling! You don't need a license or a federal inspection in order to put up a website and start offering cut-rate publishing! Be a savvy consumer. If you are writing a check *you are the boss*. Repeat that ten times, right now! Keep that in mind. Post it on your monitor, written on a sticky-note. It's your book, it represents you, the author, and just as you would not go to a job interview wearing dirty sweats, you don't want to present your readers with something that looks like a high school project. Make sure that the person you pay to publish your book earns his or her pay and does it professionally and well. Spend your dollars wisely. Educate yourself. Even if you don't intend to do the technical work of page design, covers, or formatting yourself, you'll find plenty of online articles that will explain what good page design is, or what makes a good cover.

Read those articles. Take notes. Hey, this is a lot less demanding than learning how to actually *do* the page design or format the ebook! Learn what makes a good cover. Learn what makes a lousy cover. You don't want to be yet another of those sheep getting shorn by the scammers who deliver a shoddy book to naïve authors who don't know any better! The internet is a sea of information, folks. Google is your friend! If you're going to pay someone to do the work for you, make sure you're paying for good work and make sure you know what good work is.

If your subsidy publisher is going to put your book up onto the online sites such a Amazon.com and/or make it available to the public on their site, they will pay you a royalty and keep the production cost of each book plus some profit for themselves for each book sold. The royalty you earn should be large. It should not be at the levels paid by a small-press house that did not charge you fees to publish and is actively building a loyal readership and promoting your work. Lulu Publishing, for example, tells you what the cost to you will be for each book printed for a purchaser. That cost will vary, depending on whether you include pictures and graphics, what kind of layout you choose. You then set your cover price to earn the profit level that you desire.

Small-Press: Sharing the Load

Okay, you want more than just that bucket-list publication or the family memoir. You want to publish more than once, but the idea of doing All That Work to publish and promote as an Indie author makes you break out in hives. Or it's a matter of write or promote, you only have an hour a day of spare time!

That legitimate small-press publisher is probably your best option. This is the publisher who really does plan on making money from your book, rather than making money only from the fees you pay to have your book published, as the subsidy publishers do. This publisher is selective. If your book is poorly written it will get rejected. If it will not please lots of readers, it will get rejected. These publishers want quality, rather than quantity. They want books with commercial market appeal. The will not charge you fees for set up and production. A very few will offer an advance against future royalties, the way the big legacy publishers do, but don't expect it. Many of these new, young publishing houses are hungry, working hard to build a readership and a strong catalog, and are excellent options for the new authors who simply are not ready to go it on their own.

What do you look for in a small-press publisher? You want one that publishes a limited number of titles. This can range from perhaps 5 – 20 titles a year, where one or two editors are doing all the work, to a few dozen titles a year, if the house includes several editors. Realize that quality editing takes a lot of time. This is why professional editing is usually the biggest cost of any book. It takes a lot of thought and work to make the book as good as it can possibly be without altering the author's voice or intentions. When you see a publisher churning out 300 or so titles a year, it's likely that the editing is minimal, probably no more than casual spell-checking, that this publisher is making money from fees, not from trying to make your book as strong and engaging as it can by. If they aren't making the real money from sales, why should they care if the book is any good? And never mind what they promise you. You're in a used car lot here, remember? Pay attention to what they actually deliver. Ignore those hand-picked examples of 'typical success' on the publisher website. Find people who were published by this house and are not mentioned on their home page as Shining Examples. Again, Google is your friend. Enter that publisher's name and see what pops up. Unhappy people tend to air their grievances online.

Find out where and how that publisher distributes its books. Certainly, they will be available on the publisher's website. Where else? Amazon.com, at least? Will the publisher turn them into ebooks as well? If not, do you have the right to publish the ebook version with another publisher so that you can cash in on that market as well? What rights does that publisher expect to acquire? That is very very important. We'll be talking about rights and what you need to protect, later on. But do make sure that you know what rights this publisher is acquiring before you agree to any relationship or sign any contract!

Find out what you will earn. If the publisher charges you no set-up fees or production fees, you can expect a royalty rate for print books that is more in keeping with legacy rates, but usually a bit higher since they offer no advance; say 8% to 12% of the cover price. Remember that the 'net price' or wholesale price is going to be about half of the cover price, so a really nice looking royalty of 15% of net price doesn't look quite so good when you realize that it translates into 7% of the cover price. Used car lot, remember?

If you are paying for production, you should expect to make a higher royalty on each book, at least 10% -- 20% of the cover price. For most publishers, you're going to be paying a hefty chunk of the net profits to the publisher, so you want to make sure that you're getting something in return, such as promotion, or an established pool of readers who will give your book a serious look.

Make sure you have some kind of exit strategy! The publisher may look great when you first decide to publish there, but things change. Maybe that publisher found that the business took too much time and didn't earn enough to pay the bills. So the website languishes, the book sales languish, and you decide you should take the book elsewhere or make the plunge into Indie and do it yourself.

Can you get the book back?

We'll talk about this at length in our 'rights' discussion, but you do need to have an agreement, in writing, that either you or the publisher can terminate the agreement at specified times or under specific circumstances (say, a written letter from you withdrawing the book). Usually, the publishing agreement is renegotiable after a set period of time, such as two years.

Going Indie; The Long Path

Okay, so you're not one of those folk who simply want to hold that published book in their hands and cross yet another item off the bucket list. You don't want to go with a publisher who will end up taking most of the profit from each book sold. You want to do it yourself! You want total control of this book, of all your books! Good for you! You love writing, you'd rather write books than do any other day-job you can think of, and your goal is to one day, one golden day, quit that day-job and live by your words.

That's a great goal and yes, while you can achieve that through the Legacy or small press publishers, Indie publishing is, in my opinion, the best path to that goal today.

Why, you say? Why not simply and persistently pursue the legacy publishers or small press?

When you first start out, you are a nobody. Readers don't know you, your sales are not likely to be very good – remember that long tail effect? If your book does suit the narrow market window of the New York publishers, yes, you can get picked up there. But should you do that? Yes, you get that golden window of *Kirkus* reviews, ads in the trade journals, and placement on the New Release shelf when the book comes out. The catch here is that this is great if you become a blockbuster best seller. You'll sell millions of copies, and even at the woefully small legacy royalty rate, you'll make good money.

Remember... we all expect to be the next blockbuster, but it's a lottery win. How many times have you won that lately? You could. Are you likely to? So, what if you don't win? It used to be you'd get your book back when it went OP, out of print. No longer. Now it's going to get put out as an ebook and they'll hold the rights forever, since it is still in print. The current NY royalty rate for ebooks from most if not all of the big publishers is worse than woeful. No help for quitting the day job there. And very likely, you are obligated by your contract to give the publisher right of first refusal. That means they get to publish your second book, if they choose to.

It's not a huge loss. You're publishing, but you're not going to make nearly as much money per book sold as you would if you had done the job yourself. If you do not go blockbuster, but chug along with those ebooks through that legacy publisher, you'd simply make several times the money selling most likely the same number of books over all, if you had published the book yourself.

It's a matter of bottom-line here.

If you publish yourself and your book does go blockbuster, guess what? New York comes knocking on your door. Now that's for blockbuster numbers, folks, you will not see any interest if you only sell two or three or five thousand copies in a year. But if your figures do start getting media attention and you're the Next Big Thing, you'll hear from them.

And now you can make the deal. Recently, a highly successful ebook author was courted by a New York publisher and was able to keep his ebook rights and only publish the print version with the publisher. As I said, the royalties for ebook sales through the big legacy publishers tend to be dismal. But New York was ready to deal. He had the upper hand. You are not cutting yourself off from the New York publishers by going Indie and these days, those publishers are watching the Indies. Indie books show up on the best seller lists more and more often these days.

Remember: readers really do not care who published that book a long as it' s good.

Sounds like a win-win doesn't it? Hold on there a moment! We're slipping back to that *Put it out there! Watch it turn into a best seller overnight!* ad copy you see, every time you open your browser.

It ain't quite that simple, folks.

The Day Job

Let's think this through. You publish your book. You upload it to Amazon.com from Create Space, their publishing platform, and put it out there as an ebook through Smashwords. Wow, it is published! You post the link on your Facebook page, you tell people on your blog, you hand out pretty printed bookmarks with the purchase information at work.

Who are you promoting the book to?

Your family and friends, right? And quite a few of them will probably buy the book.

Now what?

When was the last time you sat down at the computer to go find the next book you planned to read simply by clicking around on the internet, hmmm? How did you find your last good read? Usually, people hear about a book. A friend raves about it on his Facebook page, you see a great review of it on Goodreads and it looks interesting, the author guest-blogs on one of the blogs you read from time to time and he/she sounds interesting.

If you're not walking into the local brick-and-mortar bookstore and browsing the New Release shelf, you probably ran into the author or the author's book on some website or blog or social media site you visited.

That author does not know you personally. You are not one of that author's friends. That author is promoting his or her book beyond that circle of family and friends.

You need to do that, too.

How do you do that? Well, what are we all selling when we sell books? Think about this for a moment. We're selling adventure, right? Emotional stories that move us. Travel to exotic new places. A good laugh. A good cry.

We're selling entertainment.

Never forget that. You are selling *entertainment*. Your book is that entertainment. If you entertain strangers on your blog, on your Facebook page, on your website, those strangers will make a critical assumption; *this author is great, I bet the book is great, too!* And those strangers will buy your book. And if, yes, those strangers think your book is great, they will say so on their blog/Facebook page/website/ at the water cooler.

This is how viral marketing begins: Three people recommend your book to friends and three friends of each of them think it sounds good. That's nine new potential fans. Two of those potential fans from each of those three friends do like the book and tweet about it, blog about it, each reaching another three friends. Now we are up to nine new fans and 18 potential fans. Keep doing the math and the numbers get big very quickly, even when you begin with two or three happy new readers.

Viral marketing.

This is how you succeed as an Indie author. You need to get your fans to bring in those thousands and thousands of new readers. But just how do you get this ball rolling?

You entertain strangers. You think about who will probably like your book, what might interest them. And you start including those things on your blog, your social media site, your website. Might be dogs. Might be Kung Fu tournament schedules. Might be frogs and pictures of the stars. It all depends on who your readers are and what will bring them back to your site and, much more importantly, what will get them to send their friends to your site.

This takes time. It takes time on a regular basis. The patience of the average internet surfer is very short. If your blog is mostly silent except for the occasional post, if your website has not changed in weeks, you fall off the Edge of Attention into the Void of Invisibility. You need to put the time into entertaining those strangers who are going to like your book and recommend it to their friends who will like it and recommend it to their friends, who will like it and...

You get the drift.

This requires time management. You cannot succeed as a writer if all your time is spent blogging and posting to the media sites!

This requires time. If you are a single parent holding down a forty hour a week job with three kids under the age of twelve in the house and a disabled parent to care for, this is not likely to work for you.

This requires self discipline. *It is a day job.* You will not succeed if you wait for the muse to move you before you sit down to write the next book or promote this one. That fifteen minutes writing in your bathrobe before heading downstairs to a leisurely breakfast and a day of yachting is a very nice dream. By all means hope for it! But today, right now, you are on a deadline and it's a deadline that you have created and only you can enforce. You may not feel like doing it today, but you *need* to do it today. You have to be the demanding boss and the employee all at the same time.

If this will not work for you, if you're willing to give too many other things such as friends, sports, social obligations, or a spotless house, a higher priority, don't take this path. You're going to have to put writing and promotion – this day job – ahead of just about everything else. If you simply can't do that, if you feel that the writing career has to come last, after a long string of daily obligations, you will probably never see the sales that you need in order to make a sustainable income happen. It's not likely that you can quit your day job to pursue this new career, so writing time and promotion time will eat just about every hour that you are not at your day job. What are you willing to give up to give yourself that time? TV? Facebook updates? Attending every one of your kids' afterschool events? Yoga classes every evening?

Be realistic about what you are actually capable of doing and if you know that you never have been able to work on your own without direction, then this is probably not a path that will lead you to success. We will certainly take a much deeper look at the realities of time management a bit later in this book. I started my career as a single mom with two young kids and believe me, I became by necessity a master of time management!

Remember, when you choose the Indie path, you are opening a business rather than accepting a nine-to-five desk job. You're going to work awfully hard to achieve that goal of the sustainable income and a nice dinner out. Keep that goal clearly in mind. In order to achieve that goal, you're going to eat a lot of Ramen, spend a lot of your free time at the computer, and say no to some fun things you've gotten used to doing regularly, at least for the foreseeable future.

Make sure you are up for it.

The Numbers Game: How Long Do I Have to Eat Ramen Anyway?

So how soon will this work-your-butt-off austerity plan pay off for you? When can you quit the day job?

Let's face it folks, some things have not changed. Back when I was breaking into the publishing world, all of us hungry, aspiring authors had lovely dreams about the money we'd make from our books, once that publishing company accepted the manuscript. Oh yes! Clearly authors were rich, clearly that book they wrote in the den in their bathrobe (just before heading out to the yacht club) paid all the bills with plenty left over. Once that book sold, we could pay the bills and maybe even eat out sometimes!

Oh, was it a rude awakening when I actually found myself publishing in the real world! Advances for new writers were in the low four figures and they kept getting lower. Since the books didn't stay in print long unless you caught the brass ring and vaulted to best-seller stardom, you often didn't even earn out your advance. If you did earn out, your numbers might not be high enough to keep you in print. You were going to write a lot of stuff to pay the bills or keep your day job. Many authors I knew had two or three different names and wrote for the romance or erotica or whatever market as well as their main genre, to keep the income up. I wrote both mystery and SF, myself, and published a ton of short fiction in markets that actually paid reasonable money for stories. I taught writing. You weren't going to pay the bills until you were at least a solid midlist writer and that generally took two or three books to accomplish...if you made it at all. Many authors never got beyond that first couple of books, didn't have the sales to remain with the publisher, and had to come back as a 'new' author with a new name.

That's reality. It never failed, though, that whenever I told someone I was a publishing writer, they immediately assumed I was rich. Boy, I wish! But, hey, that's what I expected when I was starting out! And that's what the average aspiring writer today expects – the money will be good, once you publish.

Unless you catch that brass ring, you're going to have to work at making enough money to make the day job unnecessary, even if you're willing to live lean. Let's look at the numbers so that you get a bit of a reality check going into this business, okay? Let's say that you choose to take the ebook path to begin with. You will add print books to this later on, but for our little example here, we'll stick with ebooks. You bring out your first book and start promoting yourself effectively. You've priced your book at $3.99; not bargain basement, but lower than the established names, so you are attractive to new readers, and it earns you the maximum percentage from the ebook markets; Apple, Kindle, and Nook. That means you get an average of about $2.70 for each book sold. (That is way more than I ever earned per book with the New York publishers, by the way, and way more than any writer will earn with them, now!)

You have written a good book. You are promoting effectively. You do some promotional giveaways and 99 cent sales at the start to get folk interested, so let's say that by the end of the year, you have done pretty well for a new and unknown author and you have actually earned that $2.70 on 1500 downloads of your book. That's not great but it's not woeful, either, for a new author in the first year. So your income from that book is $4050. Dunno about you, but I need a bit more than that to live on!

But you keep up with the promotion, people like your book, and you work on Book Two. Don't figure your hourly wage. You can make more pumping gas or cleaning motel rooms! We all gotta pay these dues, folks! Anyway, in your second year, you release Book Two pretty early in the year. This year, you sell 3500 copies of book one and 4500 copies of Book Two, not including any giveaways and 99 cent sales you do for promotional purposes. That gives you a total of 8000 books sold. This year you earned 21,000 dollars.

You are getting there, aren't you? And you're working on Book Three. Hmm. Your hourly wage is improving! You might make as much per hour as you would working at a convenience store! Book Three comes out in your third year. And of course, you are still promoting. Now, however, your readers are promoting for you, too! They are telling their friends about the book, posting reviews on their blogs, liking your Facebook page. But let's not get carried away. We'll keep your growth in sales modest. This year, you sold 4500 downloads of Book One, 6000 downloads of Book Two, and 5000 downloads of Book Three. Want me to do the math? We have a grand total of 15,500 downloads. That is 1300 downloads per month, on average. This year, the IRS pricks up their ears. You earned $41,850.

How much do you need to pay your bills and live comfortably? Forget the yacht. What will work for you for as an income? You need to decide what that number is, you need to make that your financial goal. And you need to remember that people who do not promote their work sell maybe ten to 100 copies in a year. That will not earn you the numbers I am quoting here. Keep that in mind when you think about all the things you really should be doing instead of writing that next book and promoting this one! There *is* money in it for you – if you put in the work.

And you are going to need to continue to put books out there! Your sales build in part because you have more books for readers to buy. But don't get too much in a rush! Remember that every reader can be a reviewer these days. Slapping three shoddy books a year up onto your website is not the way to boost your sales through viral marketing – not if the readers are posting negative reviews on their Facebook pages! But do aim for at least one good book a year. You can do that for sure!

There's no guarantee that you will get to the numbers I mentioned in three years. It might take you four, or five, or six. You might never get there if your books are poorly written and produced. *Readers have to like them enough to tell their friends about them.* You will never get there if you don't promote yourself. These numbers are for a *good* book that engages readers easily and entertains lots of people and they are hardly best-seller numbers! I know authors who are selling way more downloads per month of their books than I have cited here, and I know authors who are selling far fewer. You must offer a good book! You must promote! You must keep writing more books! And yes, we'll cover these things thoroughly here, don't worry.

You will not be shopping for a yacht unless you snag that blockbuster brass ring, but you can work up to a sustainable day-job income if you are willing to treat your writing like a *business* and do the work. You're gonna eat Ramen for a few years, but there is an end to that other day-job in sight.

CHAPTER 4

The Bottom Line: A Good Book!

S urf around the internet today and you'll find dozens of bloggers talking knowledgably about publishing trends, numbers, promotion, sales, giveaways, and the best social media platforms for self-promotion. There's a strong sense that it's really all about promotion and if you just do that job right, the day-job-income apple will fall, splat, right smack into your lap. It reminds me a bit of that scam-publisher ad copy: '*Just slap it up there and become a best-seller! Guaranteed!*' Only this version is: '*Just slap it up there and promote it well and become a best-seller. Guaranteed!*' Indeed, if you are an effective marketer, you work hard at it and use your tools effectively, you can expect to see some pretty nice sales figures at the start. I've watched several hard-marketing authors boast about very strong sales numbers right off the bat. But then they plateaued. Pretty soon they were moaning about how the Indie revolution was over.

Hmm. Maybe. But I actually downloaded ebook copies of a couple of their novels. They were well copy-edited, without too many typos, and well produced. But the stories were weak. The characterization was about as thin as a comic book in one, and the other had some serious structural issues with a long, meandering fantasy plot. Ho hum. *Booorrring....* I don't plan to buy any more books written by either author.

Let's review that viral marketing process, shall we? You promote your book and a bunch of people read it. Some of them like the book and post glowing praise on their Facebook Pages and blogs. Some of their friends read the book, a bunch of them like it, and they... Hold on! Stop right there! *Some of them like the book... Glowing praise...* When was the last time you rushed out to buy a book after you read a friend's post, *'I read it last week, but I didn't finish it. I just couldn't get into it...'* or *'I read it and it was okay, but the characters were kind of, you know, flat...'* Hey, this is my friend, I usually like the books she likes, so why should I buy a book that I probably can't get into either? And I hate books with flat characters!

In the old days, a bad review in *Kirkus* or *The New York Times Review of Books* hurt your sales. Today, a negative review on a reader's Facebook page or blog hurts your sales just as much. If that review had been glowing, that viral progression of one reader begets two, who beget three, who beget six, might have continued. Not so now.

Without that added boost from a continuously increasing fan base who are busily telling their friends how much they like your books, and thus promoting them at no cost to you in terms of time or money, all the slick marketing in the world will not give you big sales numbers that continue to increase.

Readers have to love your book.

Readers have to love your book.

Say it with me, please, class....

Readers have to love your book!

Yes, *you* love your book! Of course you do. You would not have put all that time into it if you didn't love the characters, love the world they inhabit, love your plot. What many novice authors do not realize is that while your book will always work for you, and maybe even for your family and good friends (And would they admit it if it did not? Really?), it may not work very well for people who are not you.

That, folks, is where craft comes in.

Publishing The Slush Pile

In the Old Days of publishing, the big legacy publishers were the gate keepers. That is, the new authors sent their books to the agents or editors. They landed in a big 'slush pile', a stack of queries and manuscripts on the desk (and often the floor), waiting for some attention. The reader – the agent or editor – gave each one a quick look-over. *Is it something a lot of folk want to read? Is it well written? Does it suit the needs of my publishing house or an editor I can sell it to?* Those manuscripts that earned a 'yes' in all those check boxes got that wonderful 'we'll take it' letter. Those who did not earn a check in all those boxes got a 'thanks but no thanks'. Those books that sold moved on through the publishing pipeline. A full time professional editor made that book as strong as it could be, the copy-editor made sure there were no little logic errors, caught typos, and checked for spelling errors. The marketing department and art department came up with a cover that would attract that browsing reader looking for the next good read in the bookstore and designed the pages to look professional and be easy to read. The author got presented with a 'fix these things' letter from the editor, asking for any significant content changes (a professional editor does not change content significantly, just tweaks content to make it stronger and asks the author to make larger changes). Eventually, with the help of editor, copy-editor, marketing, and art department people, the book was ready for the bookstore shelf.

The outcome of all this was a book that had a: been selected as 'best' from that pile of manuscripts on the floor was b: made stronger with the help of the professional editor, c: cleaned up to eliminate typos and spelling errors and d: packaged in an eye-catching form for marketing.

This is what you pay for when the publisher gets all but sixty-four cents of that $7.99 paperback. Yep. If you get an 8% royalty on a legacy-published paperback, you are earning 64 cents for every book you sell. The publisher keeps the other $7.35. And they keep that $7.35 for every book you ever sell through them, even if your earnings have paid them back for every dime they ever spent on producing your book. But, your book, when it hit the bookstore shelf, was a good book to begin with, well-edited, attractively packaged, and looked utterly professional.

Today, all kinds of book end up on the bookstore shelf in our virtual bookstores. You know all those manuscripts that were stacked up on the desk and piled on the floor in the agent's or publisher's office? Well, a whole lot of them are now available on the internet bookstore sites. Got rejected by a publisher? Don't want to face those 'will they reject it' butterflies? No problem! Just go publish it yourself! I don't know about you, but I'm hearing those screaming scammers again...

Bottom line? We are publishing the slush pile. Where before, that agent or editor decided if a book was 'good' or 'not good', today, we let the readers decide. We put those books out there and readers vote with their credit cards and their blog posts. The good ones get readers, the readers tell all their friends how wonderful the book is, and it begins to take off. Yes, you have to promote it in order to get the book in front of those readers who are going to spread the word in the first place, but it's the quality of the book itself that will propel that viral spread of *'you gotta read this!'*.

Today, unfortunately, many enthusiastic, aspiring new authors, overlook this hard reality. They *love* their books and they just know that everybody will love them just as much. Unfortunately, not all the enthusiasm and hope in the universe can make readers love a book that does not engage them, that does not entertain them, that does not make them love the characters.

And we're back to craft.

The Nature of Craft

So just what are we talking about here? What do you actually need in order to engage readers and publish that quality read? What is a good book?

A good book is one that makes the readers see everything that you see when you read your book, your characters are just as real to them as they are to you, they care just as much about those people as you do, and they're dying to find out what happens to them, just as you are.

Easy, right? You just write what you love and bingo! Readers engage.

Well...not really. It's not quite that simple.

Remember...you will always see things clearly, hear character tone of voice, see the action, know exactly what every person's motivations are as the story unfolds. What no novice author really comprehends at first – and I was just as guilty of this as any other newbie writer when I started out – is that readers do not know what is in your head. You think that what *you* are experiencing as you read that scene is exactly what the readers are experiencing, but it's not. They only experience what is on the page. You are using what is on the page to evoke what is in *your* head. You don't need many details on the page since you can see the scene so clearly. But when your readers read the same scene, knowing nothing about that world inside your head, they find the scene you can see so clearly to be spotty, with huge blank spots, people who seem to be a voice only, without physical form. They find themselves unsure of where they are. *We were just in the kitchen, but now he's forking hay to the horses? Wait a minute now...* And characters can seem thin, cardboard, without the reality that lets us care about them as people. They're real to *you*, quite rich and three-dimensional, but alas, only two dimensions ended up on the page.

Or maybe you love details, you adore your characters and their world, their clothes, their furniture, rugs, pets, the landscape around them. Just to make sure that your readers enjoy it as much as you do, you include every little detail, describing the scenes meticulously, making sure that you recount the character's entire life story, the history of the family, the city, the local politics. Not one reader will have a single question about anything! They are all answered! Alas, all sense of where the story is going has vanished in this rich flood of brocades and gate-legged tables, apples and pears ripening on trees, the lineage of the local kings and their blood ties to the rulers of the rest of the small kingdoms that dot this low-lying country, and...

Help, the readers are drowning!

So what do you do to make that book work for your readers?

The Golden W (or is it an A?)

Yes, you can learn to tell a good story well, and you need to do that before you slap that book up there. Nobody is born with the ability to sit down and write a knock-your-socks-off book the first time they give writing a try, any more than a ten year old sits down at Grandma's piano for the first time and plays a concert-quality Mozart concerto.

I remember that 'born to be a writer' myth. It was pretty popular, back when I was a kid. Maybe it still is, I don't know. The myth was that you couldn't learn how to write well, you just did it, and your genius would out. Or not. You were either born a Hemingway or you were not and you should go become a secretary or a plumber or something.

Oh, *please.*

I had an English teacher in high school who informed me, very kindly, that I should choose another career path because I was not Born A Writer. I guess you had a golden W on your forehead if you were. Or maybe it was an A for author? She wouldn't tell me what the magic sign actually was, unfortunately. I could have tried to fake it if I'd known. Maybe glitter? Magic marker?

I wish I had her address, today. I would send her a single copy of every published work I have, shipped by air freight, Collect on Delivery. Let's see, that's several good-sized shipping boxes of books, anthologies, magazines, hardcover collections, paperback anthologies, foreign translations… Those hardcovers weigh a lot! The bill will get her attention for sure! But darn, I still don't see that golden W in the mirror. Or maybe it's an A. Oh well.

I've also run into a few writers who go around telling folk to 'just write it, don't revise' and get as much stuff out there as you can. I guess you throw the stuff at the wall and hope some of it sticks. What fun! Revision is so much work! It's much more fun to move onto the next story and hope you do better! Woohoo! Love this advice!

You know what, folks? If I pay money for a book, even if it's a cheapie little $1.99 ebook by a newbie author who managed to hook me with the cover and blurb and it's awful, as in poorly written, as in really poorly written, I am not doing to throw another $1.99 down that particular rat hole. Yeah, maybe he'll learn how to write, but I'm not holding my breath. Remember that viral model? Now I don't post 'this is awful' reviews on my blog or Goodreads or Facebook. Everybody can make a mistake and learn from it. But I sure won't tell people to read the book and I sure won't go back and try that author again, unless I hear from someone whose taste in books I trust that another book by that author is Really Really Good.

Lots of people are like me. And others *will* post that really scathing, really awful review of the book on Amazon.com or their Facebook page or their blog.   'Throwing it up there' is a good way to start eliminating readers if it doesn't stick. And you know what, all you new, unpublished writers that nobody yet knows? *You cannot afford to do that.* You simply cannot. No matter what anybody tells you. Learn how to do it *well*, or pay someone to edit your book professionally. Put some time or money or both into producing books that engage readers, that get you the 'really good book' reviews that set you up for that lovely viral path.

Editor or DIY?

Do you need professional editing if you're publishing yourself? Every commercial publisher is going to edit your book before it goes out for sale under the name of that publishing house. They are building their own reputations – they publish good books and readers know they can trust a book published by this house. The legacy publishers paid for it from that lion's share of your cover price that they retained. It is the most expensive part of book production, unless you get Picasso (or his ghost) to paint you an original work for your cover.

And, it's the most bang for your production buck.

Remember, you won't get those critical 'this is a great book' reviews from your readers if they don't love the book. Nobody tells all their friends to buy the book for the great cover, even though the story itself is poor. What a good, professional editor will do is to make the book *you* wrote stronger. Remember that your goal is to have readers get everything from that book that you do; the sense of characters, the great visual here and now, the gripping plot. A good editor will make that book its absolute best.

I am a good, professional editor, and I guarantee you that I can make your book better than you can make it on your own. Why? Because I am not you, I do not see anything on that page except what you put there, and I have worked on so many stories and memoirs, in so many genres, from so many writers, that I am able to see how to make *this* story better rather than to try and turn it into the type of story I usually read or the type of story I think it should be. (Which is what many peer critiquers will try to do). When I was publishing with the New York publishers, I was already a pretty good writer, publishing regularly in the top short fiction magazines. And I learned a lot from my book editors, who were very good professional editors. Good as I was, they could and did make my stories a lot better for a lot more readers.

And as a professional editor, I really should tell you all that yes, you must get professional editing if you want your self-published book to be good and sell lots of copies, shouldn't I?

Well, yes maybe you do need my services and maybe you can do fine without 'em. Boy, am I a terrible salesman, huh? Let's talk about this reader engagement and success thing. Because we're talking success and not perfection here. I can make your book better. If your skills as a writer are weaker than you realize, I can make your book a lot better. And you'll learn to be a better writer in the process, because I just can't stop teaching writing, so unless you tell me shut up, I'll teach you how to improve the next book as I improve this book. Hey, the stronger you are as a writer when you write the first draft, the stronger the book will ultimately be. I'm a reader first and I want strong, compelling new books! But readers are forgiving to some degree. I read and enjoyed a lot of books as a young reader that, craft-wise, make me cringe now. They're not all that well written, but as a 14 year old, it was the story that engaged me and while the characters didn't seem very real, hey, they had a little more substance than Cinderella or Hansel and Gretel, so that was a step up.

You see popular books where the craft is, uh, mediocre to say the least. But that story has engaged a lot of readers.

Doesn't that mean that there's no reason to worry about quality? Just slap it up there and it'll be a best-seller?

Maybe. Maybe, when you buy the next lottery ticket you'll win the jackpot. Do you want to finance the rest of your life on that ticket purchase? I don't know about you, but I am not taking out a mortgage on the strength of that lottery jackpot I am going to win.

What I am saying is that for every poorly written series that goes blockbuster you have tens of thousands of books of similarly poor quality that sold ten copies last year. Okay, maybe fifteen. And remember...what will readers post on those blogs and Facebook pages if they *don't* forgive that poor writing, the thin characters, the weak plots? Hmmm? I have an awful lot of clients and students who slapped that first book up there, saw woeful sales, and are now either learning how to write well or paying to have the next book turned into something that engages and compels readers. It's your option, but throwing it against the wall to see if it sticks is going to cost you readers if it does not. And learning how to do this craft well is going to lay the foundation for long-term career success.

You simply will not succeed if you cannot write a compelling story, whether that's fiction or memoir. Learn how to do it well, or pay someone to do it well.

Learning How

So how do you learn to write? Well, you'll find a million books on the 'how to' of writing in the virtual and brick-and-mortar bookstores. The number is mind-boggling. Some are quite good, others just tell you how this blockbuster author wrote his books and those techniques may or may not work for you. Some are just plain awful. Who *are* these people and have they ever really published anything that anyone wanted to read? So how do you find quality books on craft? Search for reviews of books on writing posted by other aspiring authors or by writing teachers. Read a variety of these books and weigh that conflicting advice you'll undoubtedly get, comparing what this author tells you to do and not do, to what that author tells you. Here's a rule of thumb for you; if the author tells you that there is *only* one way to do something, move on to another book. You can tell a good story many many ways. Oh, you'll learn lots of 'rules'. And those 'rules' have value. But they do not mean 'never ever do this'. What they actually mean is 'if you do this, you will find it very difficult to successfully engage readers'. And you will. I'll be honest with you, it's not likely that you will successfully engage readers when you break those rules as a novice writer. Remember – the story will work for *you*. Always. It's the other 30,000 or so people who really matter. So, those 'rules' are a very good and helpful guideline to you as a new author. Hey, if you're a first time skier or white water canoeist do you head for the advanced slope or the Class Five rapids? No, you probably start out with a beginner slope and a calmer river until you master your techniques.

The same thing applies to your writing technique, your craft. If you write, read, and analyze good writing, you will get better. That's what those 'rules' mean; Advanced Slope! Class Five Rapids Ahead! So when the author of a book on writing tells you; *You must never do this!* that person is telling you that you will never master your craft. Wow. What kind of attitude is that? You can break every rule out there, as long as you obey the one iron-clad rule of writing: *The story must work for 30,000 strangers.* Ahem, notice that '30,000 strangers'? That's the catch. Remember. It will *always* work for you. So put some serious time into mastering your craft if you don't want to shell out for the services of a professional editor.

Read, read, read. That does not mean that you should chow down on popular best-sellers. Yeah, they're best sellers, but alas, in most cases, it is not the quality of the writing that catapulted them to best-seller status. Nearly every one of our popular best-sellers is pretty flawed in terms of craft. Why not learn from them? you ask. They became best-sellers! Yeah, but you can't duplicate the reason they reached best-seller status. You can copy King, Grisham, Nora Roberts, and Rowling 'till the cows come home – and many authors have done so – and your sales will likely be modest at best.

Nobody has yet figured out what it is that turns this author, this series, into a best-seller. And believe me, many many many people have worked hard at it! Scan the reviews and read books that several quality reviewers agree are very well written books. Pay attention to what gets praised. Is it a powerful plot that earns that praise? Powerful characterization? When you read a book for pleasure and find yourself completely sucked into the story, analyze your own reaction. *What makes me love this story?* Do you love the vivid and charming characters? The powerful and creepy milieu that has you jumping every time the furnace comes on? Is it the intricate and complex plot that surprises you when you think you know just where the story is headed? Take that story apart and pay attention to just how the author brought those characters to life. Outline that complex plot for a sense of how that author structured it to make it surprising without confusing readers. Pay close attention to the language and word choices that the author used in his or her description to create that powerful here and now. Read for pleasure first and then dissect the books that impact you to learn from them. Were you bored to tears? Figure out why. This is what you do not want to do in your own writing, for sure!

Your best bet is to write what you love to read. You may not be able to tell me why that mystery worked and this mystery wasn't that good, but you know 'good mystery' when you read it, if you're a mystery lover who reads a lot of mysteries. If you sit down to write your own mystery, you'll start out with a 'feel' for where the story should go, what the characters need to do in order to satisfy readers like yourself. Same thing for romance, science fiction, young adult, or any other genre. If you read it all the time, you have a good feel for what will satisfy readers.

Editor Shopping

Okay, you've decided that life is too short, you hate to take classes, you don't have a critique group around that you want to join, you just want to write the darn books and get them up there. So you're going to pay for a professional editor.

This is a best choice for a lot of novice writers. As an editor, I can fix things in a book that might take that writer a couple of years of hard learning to fix on their own. It costs money up front, and it's not cheap. It takes a *lot* of hours to do it right! The hard part for the novice author is finding an editor who does a good job. Anybody can call themselves an editor and many do. I've had mediocre writing students who were far from writing compelling fiction when they took the course I was teaching, but who, within months of finishing the course, were advertising themselves as editors and charging clients money to edit their books. Whew! All I could do was to shake my head and hope that their potential clients did their homework.

I've had more than one client cry on my shoulder because they paid someone to 'edit' their book and that person did a terrible job. Or, in one case, pirated the work. A professional job of editing is going to cost you from one thousand to several thousand dollars. I price on the low side of that scale, because I want as many authors as possible to be able to take advantage of good editing (I'm a reader first and I want good books!) and I'm not looking to get rich. If the price seems too good to be true, it is. Believe me, folks, serious editing is a slow slow process and you really do have to be more than just an author. A good editor can handle only a limited number of books a year. There are only so many hours in a day.

Google is your friend. Look for blog posts including this person's name or ask for references from clients this person has worked for. Do realize that an editor cannot turn a weak story into a best seller. That editor can only make that weak story as strong as it possibly can be. You're not looking for the editor who always turns out a best seller. That editor does not exist, not even among the legacy publishers whose editors make pretty impressive salaries. But you want an editor who is familiar with the genre you write in (this is very important), and who does more than simply catch typos and fix grammar errors. Remember those books I read, after the authors complained that their sales had plateaued? Someone had fixed all those grammar errors and caught all those typos and the stories were still boring and weak. Typo-fixing is copy editing, not content editing. You want content editing.

Your editor will bring your craft up to professional level, even if you are woeful at dialogue or description or what have you. It is also your editor's job to make the content stronger. Professional editors do not make content changes to your manuscript – you are the author, it's your story, and you need to make those changes. But it is the editor's job to show you where you need to make changes. It is the editor's job to let you know when you violate your characterization, when your dramatic arc falters, when the scenes are confusing to readers or are simply weak and boring. It is your editor's job to tell you how to make this story as strong as it can possibly be. That is rarely a matter of merely catching grammar errors and fixing typos.

You're going to pay a lot of money for this service, so make sure you are getting good service. And then pay the money. Remember – you won't take that viral path if you don't have a good book. When you do take that viral path, you'll earn back the money you spent to make that book as good as it can be. And unlike the legacy system where you pay for those services forever by giving the publisher the lion's share of the cover price, once you've earned back the money you spent on editing, the money you earn from then on is all profit for you. Editing, for the Indie author, is a one-time up-front cost. It's not a lifetime mortgage on the book.

Do realize that a good author is not automatically a good editor. In fact they rarely are. Most authors only know how to make a book work the way they make their books work. A friend of mine handed his nonfiction book to another friend who is a professional science writer. His book was not intended for that market, it was an owner-friendly how-to on dog training intended for the pet-owner market. That author tore the book apart, insisting that he structure it the way she structured her well-published science articles. It ruined the book and more importantly, it so discouraged the author that he abandoned what would have been a highly marketable project. She simply did not understand how to make that book work for a different market than the one she wrote for. She did not understand the difference in reader expectations between the readers of *Science Magazine* and the dog owner at the pet store, looking for an entertaining and informative book about dog training.

The bottom line here is that you need to produce a good book. You either need to learn how to write a strong and compelling book, or you need to pay someone who can help you make your book as strong and compelling as it can be. There is no way around this. A Good Book is the foundation upon which your publishing success is built. If your foundation is weak, success is not all that likely.

Remember, we're publishing the slush pile. This is one thing that has not changed since I first began writing: You need to rise to the top of the slush pile!

CHAPTER 5

Taking The Path

O kay, you've made your decision. You have a good book, you want that writing career and you're opting to start the business rather than take that 9 to 5 desk job. Good for you! You're going to keep total control of your work, you get to decide how hard you want to work at making this business a success, and nobody can trip you up by making bad marketing decisions about your books. Oh, sure, you can make bad decisions or fail to do the work, but then you'll know right where to lay the blame, won't you?

First things first. You're going to start promoting your book. Now.

What? Oh, yes, I can hear you. *I can't promote my book! I'm not even done with the first draft yet!*

Yeah? So? Remember -- nobody knows who you are yet. You know that long tail I talked about earlier? You're going to start off with one fan, who will hopefully beget two or three, and each of them will hopefully beget two or three... You know. That viral path to success. So why not start now? Why not start introducing your future readers to your characters, your world, that great story idea? Why not show them that you are an entertaining writer, whether it's the story or memoir you're working on or that tale of the off-the-wall encounter with a childhood friend at the doctor's office you posted to your blog? There is nothing more satisfying and more valuable to your career than putting your book into the virtual bookstores and seeing really good sales numbers in the first weeks. And that won't happen unless readers have discovered you and think your book is probably a pretty good read. It's fine to post scenes on that website or blog. By all means post all that backstory and world building stuff that you can't really include in the book without bogging down the story. Find images of people who look like your characters that you can post. Take pictures of the setting, if your book is set in the real world. We all know tons more about our characters and our world than we can include in the book. The website is a great place for it! And besides, promotion is so much more than just talking about your book.

In fact, promoting yourself and your work is a huge topic all on its own and we'll get that topic a bit later. In detail. In great detail!

Choosing Your Publishing Platform

You're working on your promotional platform and finishing up the draft of the book. It's time to talk about just how and where you are going to publish it. Options abound. You can publish it as an ebook first, then bring it out in print form. You can publish it only as a print book or only as an ebook, or you can publish it as an ebook and a print book together from the get-go. Let's talk about what is involved in each of those two options.

Ebooks are relatively easy to format, unless you're a complete techno-phobe and will suffer an asthma attack if you so much as read a set of 'how to' instructions. They are quite inexpensive to produce yourself. That is, you can format the book, create a cover for it, and upload it to any or all of the ebook platforms; Kindle, Nook, Sony, and Apple at no cost to you but your time and without purchasing any expensive software. If you pay someone to do the work of formatting and upload the book for you, it'll cost you some money but not as much as editing will. You know what? It'll probably take you quite a few hours to do the formatting yourself the first time, especially if you have no experience with html or xhtml, but really, anyone can do it. Quite a few tech-naïve students and clients of mine have slogged through the process, done quite nicely, and survived to tell the tale. You can, too. Hey, if it takes you 20 hours to format that first book and you would have had to pay a publishing service $300 that you can't afford to do it for you, you've just earned $15 an hour, since you saved that $300. That's not a great hourly wage, but hey, if money is tight, you can make it work. If you're going to publish ebooks regularly I really suggest you tough it out, slog through it, and learn how to format your own ebooks. If you simply don't want to do it, I, and many other publishing services people can do it for you.

The major platforms; Kindle, Nook, Sony, and Apple all offer publish-it-yourself gateways and tutorials that help you format and upload your book. Yes, the formatting is different for Apple products than it is for the other e-readers and yes, the formatting is different for the Kindle Fire, which is a tablet, than it is for the Kindle e-readers. It's even different – a bit – for the older Kindles than it is for the more recent Kindles that offer more bells and whistles. The Nook also has its own little differences, and then there's the Sony e-reader... Is your head spinning yet? Okay, you can stop hyperventilating now!

It is not that difficult, even if you format for each platform separately. Once you have the basic page design set up and you've gotten your feet wet formatting the ebook, it's just a matter of doing it a bit differently for each of those platforms. Or, you can publish through Smashwords. They are a rapidly growing giant of ebook publishing and they do a good job. And no, they do not charge you anything up front. They are all about self-publishing and all about ebooks. What they will do is allow you to format your ebook into an Epub file and then they will convert that file for you to work on the other publishing platforms. Instead of formatting it four or five times for individual platforms, you can format it once and their software does the rest of the work.

What's in it for them? A cut of your cover price, of course. Didn't your grandma tell you that there's no free lunch? If there is, I sure haven't stumbled over it yet. But you give them no rights and that cut is pretty reasonable considering that they'll distribute your ebook to the main electronic booksellers for you. They do their best to educate you as a novice Indie author about how to format the book properly. The book will look good to your average reader.

If you are a perfectionist and you want that ebook to look absolutely perfect on every e-publishing platform, I recommend that you purchase *The eBook Design and Development Guide* by Paul Salvette, published by BB eBooks. It is the nerd's guide to ebook formatting and publishing, and it's very well written. I actually found myself staying up late at night to finish chapters. Mr. Salvette goes into the formatting differences between the various Kindle models as well as the tablet and e-reader devices, and offers specific advice on how to make your book look perfect on every platform. Even if you plan to have someone else format your ebook, I recommend that you buy the book (it's quite inexpensive as an ebook) and read it for your own education. You will understand the formatting pitfalls and will know what questions to ask and what answers to expect as you shop for that formatting service. Remember, folks, the publishing world is entirely a 'buyer beware' universe. Nobody is required to offer you good service, no matter what they advertise. If you do not know what 'good service' is, you are at the mercy of advertising as you wander this used car lot, looking for that bargain. Once that check is cashed, it can be difficult to get your money back if you discover that while your ebook looks great on an older Kindle, it has major problems on the Fire and don't even look at it on the iPad, never mind that the person formatting for you promised that it would work on all platforms. You need to educate yourself, even if you decide that this formatting stuff is better left to the nerds.

Moving beyond formatting, let's talk page design here. That's a huge issue in print publishing, but less of an issue with ebooks. Why? Because ebook text changes to fit the page and as the readers expand or contracts it to suit their eyesight. So the 'how' of making that page look professionally published is less complex than it is when the pages don't change and you can do more to make those pages attractive and easy to read. But you will want some specifics. Take a look at well published ebooks. You'll see a few basic similarities. Each page, for example has a header that tells you what you are reading. Usually it is the title. The text contains no unexpected blank spaces. Chapters use a larger and sometimes different fonts than the text and the text is one of the easy-to-read fonts such as Times New Roman. Go to the cover. You'll find 'Front Matter' following it that includes a blurb about the book, a full title page with author name, a page that includes publisher details, ISBN, and art credits for the cover. An Acknowledgements page, thanks people who assisted the author, and/or a Dedication page may fit here. There's usually a second title page, which is followed by a Table of Contents, with internal links to take readers directly to each chapter or section. This is followed by a Forward and Introduction, if they are included, or Chapter One may immediately follow the table of contents. Following the main content of the book is the 'Back Matter', if any. This could include an Afterward, an About the Author page, including a link to the author's website and blog (a very good idea, folks!), or blurbs and cover thumbnails of other books published by that author (with 'buy' links, of course).

One of the lovely assets of the ebook is that, of course, you can include hyperlinks to websites when you publish for the web-connected readers such as the Kindle Fire or the Ipad or Iphone. But do remember that the simple ereaders may not have that capability and if your book depends on using those hyperlinks, you will disappoint readers without the ability to make use of them. Remember this when you choose where and in what form to publish that ebook and make it clear in your promotion that links to video content or websites are a big part of that book's content if they are critical. Remember that disappointed readers can post their disappointment very publicly!

Let's not forget price here. This is an important part of building that viral path. If I don't know an author at all, I may be tempted by an eye-catching cover and a really cool blurb. Hmm. Sounds good. Or I visited that author's blog and really like his or her style. I'm entertained! Surely the book will be entertaining, too, and I like that genre. But if the book is available only as a trade paperback for $14.99 or more, or the ebook is priced at $9.99, the price for an established author published in ebook format through the New York publishers, I may decide to wait and see if I run into good reviews from reviewers I trust, first. That's a considerable pile of quarters to plunk down for a book I may delete from my reader at the end of Chapter Four. But I have no problems dropping two or three or even four bucks on an ebook just to see if this author might possibly find a place on my 'favorites' list. Many authors reduce the price of their early ebooks as they publish new work, accepting a smaller profit but letting those $1.99 or $2.99 books serve as 'loss-leader' promotional material for their newer works. And don't forget sales. A week-long 'free' or $.99 sale price as a promotional tool can net you a lot of downloads. Some of those readers won't love your book, but others will and they may become fans and buy all your other books. It's much easier to reduce the price of ebooks to those temporary 'fire sale' levels than it is with print books, where you may have a production cost that must be met for each book printed.

Overall, the ebook is a good entry point for the new author. Once you have the book out there, you're seeing sales, and your promotional platform is up and running, consider adding the print version. More readers still read print books than read on e-readers. For now. And quite often, the person who loves your cover and the book will buy the print edition for the home library even though they already have the book on their e-readers. With today's print-on-demand technology, it can cost you nothing up front to upload your book for printing and get it distributed through a POD publisher such as Amazon.com's Create-Space, if you are willing to do all the work yourself.

Putting It On The Page

A professional looking printed page takes a bit more work and education than does a well-formatted and good-looking ebook. Microsoft Word is not a good publishing tool, folks. Neither is WordPerfect. You can make your book look decent without spending hundreds of dollars for Adobe InDesign or QuarkXPress, two good mid-level publishing systems out there. They cost, by the way, in the $700 - $900 dollar range and are high end products, well-supported by their companies. InDesign will also format ebooks and is used extensively for brochure and website layout, with very flexible graphics and video interface capabilities. These are not commercial publishing software platforms – those cost thousands of dollars and are highly specialized – they're intended primarily for the brochure and website designer, but they will do a good job on a print book for you and are used by many small-press publishers. If you plan on print-publishing all your books yourself or becoming a small-press publisher of other peoples' books, it is worth the money to purchase one of these software packages. Both of these packages may be available as a 30 day free trial, and I would try both to see which one works better for you. If this does not fit your budget, you can purchase one of several brands of desktop publishing software. Microsoft Publisher, which, of course, as a Microsoft Office product works quite well with Word, costs less than $150. Again, if you can get a free trial and I would do so. It is much more limited in capability than InDesign or QuarkXPress and does not include the extensive graphics, video, and e-publishing capabilities that other mid-level packages do, but it's better than the simple word processing software that probably resides on your computer.

There are a host of other desktop publishing options out there, including free content, if your budget is really tight. If you want to upload that print book to a POD publisher yourself and want the product to look professional, rather than resemble a high school term paper, turn to Google, search out and read reviews of desktop publishing software, and find something that you can afford.

Now that you have the software you need, let's talk page design. There are many books out there that deal with page design. Your choice of font, the spacing of the letters, the margins, headers, footers, chapter titles, and so on matter. We have gotten used to reading professionally produced books from big New York publishers who work very hard at page design. Few readers are aware of that aspect of publishing, but when you ignore it and simply slap that Word or WordPerfect file onto a printed page you hurt your book.

Why? Because at the back of our minds as we read, a little voice whispers 'this is homemade'. And while yes, we do like that wonderful homemade cake that Grandma bakes so well, we are a bit more prejudiced about 'homemade' when we're not talking food. Your readers will feel a bit of subconscious prejudice that this book really isn't 'a book' because the author clearly published it himself or herself. Readers don't care who published the book...as long as it *seems* professional. But when it's a 'term paper' with a lousy cover or even – and I saw a lot of this when self-publishing through the POD houses first took off – with no cover, just a title and author name on a plain page, we don't give it the same respect. Many authors choose to create their own 'publishing company' to avoid giving away the fact that they're self-publishing the book. They may never publish a book that they did not write, but the readers will see the name of a publishing company in the front matter.

If you're not sure about this format-your-own-book thing, you can find a free wiki-book on the subject, *Basic Book Design* by Thomas David Kehoe and other Wikibooks contributors. It's available as a free pdf download and covers the subject of formatting quite well. (I'm not going to endorse his evaluation of the publishing software, though). Download it and read it through. Again, even if you plan to pay someone to format and publish your book, you need to know what 'good service' means, if you expect to get it!

Cover Is As Cover Does

One of the biggest reasons for bar-stool wailing and gnashing of teeth at the big writers conferences used to be the 'bad cover'. Legacy authors had absolutely no say over their cover art. Okay, maybe if you were selling 3 million copies of every new release and could jump ship to another publisher if you didn't get your way, they'd humor you. But not otherwise. So all authors held their breath until they saw the cover sketches or the final cover flats, whichever they got to see first. Then, you either celebrated or headed for the bar to order a double and wail. Why?

Covers sell books.

Or they don't. They can turn readers off or give readers a wholly false impression of what is inside, leading readers to pass that book over on the shelf or buy it and then be disappointed. You know what disappointed readers do, right? And they do it loudly, on their Facebook pages and blogs.

What makes a good cover? Several key elements are important. The title and author name need to be readable. I cannot believe how many covers bury flowery, hard to read fonts in busy, cluttered art so that you end up squinting at the image to try and read the title. Then there are the authors who think that a spindly blue lettering looks *so* dramatic on that dark cover. Hello? Have you actually tried to read those words on your screen? Or on the cover in your hands? Red lettering on that busy image of a castle in flames doesn't work too well either. Nor does white lettering on a panoramic image of a misty meadow. You really do need to *look* at your cover. Creative 'good ideas' are not always practical.

The image needs to be clear, uncluttered. How do we see covers today? If you're publishing with a small-press publisher or doing it yourself, your reader will most likely see the cover in their browser window and it'll be a thumbnail. Lots of clutter in that cover will merge into a mishmash of color, reducing the impact of the book. Folks, the reality is that a poorly designed cover suggests to our quiet little hindbrains that the book is poorly done, too. We are very influenced by that quiet voice, even if we don't consciously notice it. Remember that this is like a job interview; just as the potential boss notices the applicant's need for a haircut and wrinkled clothes, the readers notice the book's cover and page design. Unprofessional suggests poor writing. That may not be the case, but if the readers pass on the book, nobody is ever gonna find out that the writing is good, will they?

Ideally, the cover is eye-catching and has some connection to the content. If your mystery revolves around professional basketball, a thrilling shot of someone slam-dunking the ball may be an ideal choice, or perhaps the image of a basketball dabbled in blood on the empty court floor beneath that limp basket.

Again, educate yourself. (My, isn't this a familiar theme!) Go online and look at book-covers. Look at lots of book covers. Easy to read title and author name? Clear image that doesn't confuse the eye? Does it make you want to read the blurb, find out what the book is about? Or is it just 'okay, nothing special'? Go back to Google and start looking for essays on cover design. You'll find plenty of them out there on various author and publisher blogs.

As to cover design, if you know your way around graphics software such as Adobe Photoshop or the free-content Gimp, or you have purchased InDesign for your print-publishing, by all means do the cover yourself. Learning your way around this software can be complicated and time-consuming – it's a slog, just as it is to learn ebook formatting. If you plan on publishing lots of books, it's probably worth your time to learn how to do it. If you're lucky, you have a friend who is a talented graphics artist who will do the cover for you. But do know what you want from that cover, first. A good webpage design does not necessarily make a good cover.

Yes, you can buy this service as well, and the price will range from sky-high 'art' pricing to something more along the lines of quality craft work. If you have a very specific cover design in mind, and your designer has to create the image from scratch, it's going to cost you a lot more than if that designer can simply use a couple of photo images and manipulate effects and fonts to give you want you want. Whether you buy it or take the DIY route, spend the time or money to create a good cover for your book. That is what will catch a browsing reader's eye first.

Blurb It Up!

You're going to need a short, catchy blurb for your book, no matter what platform you choose to publish in. The browsing reader is going to notice your cover or recognize your name and instantly want to know what the book is about. That blurb is usually published on the back of the paper-published book, and is posted on the book's buy-page. It's also a key feature of your promotional material.

Learn how to do it well!

A common novice mistake is to assume that the readers want a small, condensed outline of the book's entire plot. Now they'll know everything! They'll know what the book is all about. Isn't that what they want?

No.

The readers want to know if this book is going to entertain them. Does it sound exciting? Fun? Scary? Do I just have to read it right now? Or should I put it on my 'maybe one of these days' list? The readers don't want information, they want entertainment! It's your job to hook their interest with this blurb, to tickle their curiosity, to make them want to read your book right now!

Let's look at a little blurb example here. You all know this story:

One day, Goldilocks went for a walk the deep dark woods and found a little cabin. Nobody was home, but she was lost, tired, and hungry and she went inside to wait for the owners to come back. There, she found their dinners on the table and couldn't help herself! She was so hungry, she ate the smallest bowl of porridge. Afterward, she want into the living room to sit and wait for them but rocked too hard in the littlest rocking chair, breaking it. Sleepy after her meal, she went upstairs to fall asleep in the 'just-right' smallest bed, only to be rudely awakened later on when the owners of the cabin came home. They turned out to be a family of three bears and they chased Goldilocks all the way home!

Okay, now the readers know the whole story, don't they? Ho hum. Can't wait to read it...*not*. Let's sell this puppy, shall we?

Lost, frightened, hungry, Goldilocks thought she was saved when she stumbled upon the little cabin deep in the dark woods. But the owners weren't home! Too hungry for manners, she ate some of their dinner and finally fell asleep in one of the three beds upstairs. And then the owners came home. Bears do not welcome trespassers...

Imagine this now, in that dark, movie-trailer voice. It focuses on the conflict; lost girl, thinks she's found salvation. But when the cabin owners come home...they are bears! Notice that the blurb does not give away the ending? We don't know if she lives or ends up bear-dinner. The blurb leaves the readers wondering what happened. And that curiosity nudges them to go ahead and buy the book. *Sounds exciting, might be a good read!* You may have published a good book, but if readers don't read it, they can't post that glowing review of it on social media and blogs and you won't start out on that viral path. The very first steps to getting those readers to read your book are your cover and your blurb.

Time And Money: Learn It or Buy It?

You now should have a clear idea of what you'll need to do in order to put that book out in front of readers as a professional product. You'll need to design your pages well, format the book for either print or ebook publishing, upload those files to the publisher, obtain an ISBN number, arrange for distribution, come up with a good looking cover and create a catchy blurb to attract browsing readers.

Sounds pretty daunting, doesn't it?

It *is* a lot of work and if you're planning on publishing just this family memoir, it's probably not going to be worth it to you to learn how to do all of this, unless you simply want to keep total control of all aspects of the project and make the book turn out exactly the way you want it to.

Let's talk about the realities of time and money here. How comfortable are you with learning new technology? Did you have to get help to set up your new, out-of-the-box computer? Have you still not figured out how to make Word double-space your document or produce different headers and footers on different pages? Maybe you don't want to do all that book-formatting stuff. It's fine! There are many ways to pay someone else to do this for you. You can hire an editor – we talked about doing that. You have individuals who offer formatting services; they'll format your book for Create Space or the ebook platforms or one of the print-on-demand publishers such as Lulu Publishing.

You can hire someone to design you a cover. You can hire someone to write you a catchy blurb, if that seems to be beyond you. The new publishing paradigm has created a need for this type of service and people have flocked to fill that need. You've got the subsidy publishers who are willing to do everything for you; edit, design, format, and cover your book, publish it and distribute it, for a price and a share of the sales. Yes, you will pay out money up front, but if you are a wise and comparative shopper, you are going to get good services for the best price possible. If it's a good book that engages readers, if you promote it well to set your feet on that viral path, you will make money on it. And when you have made back that money you spent on all those paid-up-front services, the profits from then on are entirely yours. If you decide that you simply do not have the budget to shop for services and you cannot face the work of the DIY process, then you need to look to the commercial publishers, small-press or even New York. But realize that, because these publishers depend on your book selling many many thousands of copies in order to turn a profit, they are going to be highly selective. You are competing with well-published professionals in this arena. If your book is not professional in quality, if it interests a niche market rather than the average reader, if it's a family memoir, the publishers will probably decide the book won't sell enough copies and turn it down, even if it's a good book. Markets matter to them. You'll find that the commercial slush-pile is extremely competitive today, particularly as the Big Six publishers have contracted to become the Big Four, leaving many well-published authors looking for new homes in the small-press world.

Remember that this is a Buyer Beware universe. Not all those people advertising their services or offering to publish your book Right Now are going to do a good job for you. Once someone has your check it's very difficult to get your money back. You need to be a savvy and wary consumer. In our next section, Publishing Safely, we're going to talk about how to determine if someone offering a service is going to do a good job for you or not.

So what if you are good at one or more of the skills you need in order to publish your book, but you don't have all the skills needed to do the whole job? There's a new option out there and that is the publishing cooperative. Groups of aspiring writers have banded together to pool their skills so that they can publish their work through the group effort. Some members may have graphics skills, while someone else is a professional editor, and another author might be happy to design and format books for print or ebook production. They might take turns blogging or maintaining the website. Book View Café is one such long-standing venture, and all members share the load for the entire publishing and promotion process.

This is a great way to do things, although it does require some careful planning so that everybody does share that load and individual copyrights are carefully protected. You may find one in operation that you can join, or you may have some author friends who can pool skills with you to begin your own. It is one good way to share the time-burden of mastering those essential publishing skills that you need if you want to make it a DIY project from start to finish.

In any case, evaluate your own time and abilities objectively before you decide on your publishing choices. How much time do you have to devote to learning new skills? How many books do you intend to publish? How tight is your budget, really? These are all questions that only you can answer, and they need to be answered honestly before you can make a good choice.

CHAPTER 6

Publishing Safely

An accountant friend of mine called me one day. The family of an elderly client had come to him, worried about a lot of large charges on Dad's credit card – to the tune of several thousand dollars. The payments went to a publishing company that I will not name here, and Dad proudly told his kids that his memoir was on its way to becoming a best seller. The kids brought a copy to my accountant friend and he, a life-long reader, was not at all impressed with the typos, poor grammar, and poor writing in a book that was essentially a diary of a middle-class family man.

Best seller? Maybe not.

Turns out that a very nice young women called Dad about once a week to report on the 'progress' of the book on its way to best-sellerdom. No, it wasn't doing very well at the moment, but there was this writers conference or that one, and that would be a great place to promote the book so that it took off! They'd print and ship the books to the conference and make them available as giveaways.

For a price.

A hefty price. On top of the thousands he had spent already for editing and publishing services with this company.

But the girl was *so* enthusiastic and praised his wonderful memoir as a real masterpiece. It was only a matter of time until the book took off and earned back all that money he had spent! Surely, another thousand bucks or so for yet another promotional campaign wasn't too much to pay for an ultimate best-seller that would make him a superstar! Of course, at that point, nearly all 'sales' of his book were for these 'promotions'. He was getting a lot of phone calls from smiley and enthusiastic company reps, encouraging him to hang in there on his path to stardom.

Alas, this is a very common scenario. I left my email address on this publisher's website as a test case and got a phone call within 24 hours from a very professional sounding 'editor' who told me my 'idea' was fantastic and did I have the manuscript ready for marketing? They were *very* interested. Being an honest person, I admitted that I was a writer and editor and was simply investigating their marketing practices. The 'editor' I spoke with was 'shocked' at the details I related and vowed that a 'rogue employee' must be violating company policy. Maybe. But you know what? I got calls from that company for the next 9 months, from sincere and encouraging 'editors' wanting to know if my book was ready to submit yet. I still get the occasional email.

They seem to employ a lot of these 'rogues' who are doing a hard sell pitch to the naïve new writer. And they are targeting the elderly. My 87 year old neighbor who reads nothing but magazines and has no interest in writing got a cold call from a nice 'editor' lady who told him she knew he had a great story in him and she'd love to help him share it with the world. She was good. He was in the Coast Guard during World War II and a pilot all his life and she just about had him convinced that the world couldn't wait to read his story. He has now received three such 'you must have a good story in you and we can help' calls.

These companies are making enough money to hire talent, folks. And it's not editorial talent, believe me.

Quite a few of these scam outfits exist. They are very large, they pay for very professional telemarketers and skilled copywriters to write their ads. They know what your dreams are and they speak directly to those dreams, apparently guaranteeing them to you – for a price. Who doesn't want to believe a publisher who tells them that their book, their pride and joy, has the potential to set the world ablaze and sell a million copies? That it's a masterpiece? Oh, they have the pitch down! And let's face it, all of us, when we are new authors, are filled with those dreams and none of us at that stage, myself included when I first started writing, know enough and are objective enough, to see the sales pitch hiding beneath the sweet promise of success. Quite a few of my writing students have told me 'it's too expensive to self-publish' and then explained that it cost them four or five or six thousand dollars to publish with company A, B, or C and they've only sold 20 or 30 copies of their books...

This is why I started New Writers Interface. I hate these people. They prey on the dreams we all have for our books. They are very very good at it. Their ultimate answer, when none of those promises they've made come true, is that 'readers just don't like your book'. And so, the hopeful author is left feeling like a failure and short a few thousand bucks he or she did not need to spend. Rarely if ever are the services they provide top-quality. I've seen shoddy print production, books that seemed to be nothing more than a printed Word file without any formatting, and expensive 'promotion packages' that sent the author instructions to start a Facebook page and send a PR release to the local newspaper. The 'blog tours' that are also very expensive, seemed to cut and paste information only into the blogs of other authors published by this same scam outfit, none of which had many followers at all.

You need to protect yourself. Nobody is going to look out for the best interests of your book except you. So how do you do that? You educate yourself. That's why you're reading this book, isn't it? You learn what 'good service' is and if you're going to shell out your hard-earned cash to pay for services, you make sure that service is good and is offered at a competitive price. Yes, that ad shouting at you on your browser window promises that your book will be published today for a pittance. That's nice. Today seems a bit fast if you want quality, or at *least* a spell-check before your pages are out there for the world to see. And that price may not cover what you need. One 'bargain basement' offer to publish an ebook for cheap charged extra for formatting for each platform, the ISBN, editing, proofing, cover...the list of extra charges went on and on. It wasn't such a bargain by the time you purchased everything you needed in order to actually get the book into the online bookstores.

Lots and lots of companies offer these services and they all call themselves publishers. Well, they *are* publishers. They're going to publish your book for you. That really means nothing else. Some are good, others are not. Would you go buy a washing machine or a car at the first place you looked? Knowing nothing about the brand? I hope not. I like to find the best price when I buy things. I'm willing to pay for quality, but I want to get the best price for that quality.

Listen up! YOU are in charge. YOU are writing the check. If that publisher is taking your money in order to publish your work, that publisher is working for YOU. Never mind that 'authors and publishers share the risk today' nonsense. That may be so, but the publisher's share is to do quality work for you, in return for that check. Believe me, if that publisher doesn't offer what you want, you will find others who do. And maybe the price will even be better. Too many authors are still living with the mindset of the 'old days' where only a few aspiring authors were admitted into the 'inner sanctum' and published by the big legacy houses. They were supposed to be the cream of the crop. That acceptance letter was a thrilling experience. It meant you were good! It made you special. You were a published author! Oh, don't we all want to feel special? I sure did. I'd be lying if I said I didn't.

This 'chosen few' status is still the case if you are publishing with a commercial publisher who charges you nothing and takes only the right to publish and earn money from your book in exchange for that royalty you will get paid. That just means you have an idea that the marketing department thinks will sell lots of copies. If you pay one dollar for the publication of your book then that publisher is working for you, and you have a big say in what gets done and how. If you don't like what is offered, take your book and your money somewhere else. Anyone and everyone can (and does) publish their book in today's new publishing world. Being a published author is like saying that you printed out a draft on the printer at home. 'Good' is now measured by how many readers love your book. How well it is published and pro-moted is a big part of finding those readers who will love it. It is likely, as readers find their own next read, that the quali-ty of the production – the cover, the appearance of the pag-es – will play an increasing role in the readers' choice to read this book as opposed to that book. Poor quality produc-tion may be interpreted to mean a poor quality story, just as a non-professional-looking manuscript used to be regularly rejected without a serious look, by the legacy editors and agents.

Your book is a job interview, remember. Just as you wouldn't show up for most job interviews dressed in dirty sweats that needed a good wash, you don't want to show up on the reader's browser or on the shelf with a book that seems like a high school class project, produced on the home printer.

You are a consumer, shopping for services. And the ulti-mate success of your book may well depend on how well you shop.

Keep that in mind!

And keep in mind, too, that the job of the publishers who charge money is to make as much money from you as they possibly can. That's the job of any business-owner, right? Sell product, make money. They're not evil if they're honest. They're evil when they lie to the authors and prey on their naiveté to sell them poor quality services that they don't need anyway, with the implied guarantee of a success that is not likely to happen. Your job, as consumer-author, is to get the best service for your dollar.

You and the honest publisher will find the place to meet in the middle. That's how the market has always worked, whether you're shopping for a new car, or deciding what services you do and do not need from that publisher.

Too Good to be True

One sure sign of a scam operation – that is, a publisher who wants your money and has little interest in the success of your book in spite of their claims to the contrary – is glowing praise. *This is the next Moby Dick! You have the potential to be the next Grisham...Rowling...Nora Roberts...* (Fill in the blank with the appropriate best-selling author.) Yes, we all want to believe that! For sure! And there's that old-days mindset again; the Publishers have Special Knowledge. They Know... Well, yeah, the publishers who only get a paycheck because the books they published sold millions of copies, they *do* know what lots of people tend to buy. At least they can make an educated guess. Have you noticed that Random House and Putnam and the other big NY publishers are not sending you letters begging you to submit your manuscripts? You know why that is? Because they have more good-quality manuscripts on their desks, in their slush-piles, than they can use. They don't need yours. That overly enthusiastic 'oh, this is so wonderful, it's a sure best seller' should set a bunch of alarms sounding in your mind. And when it's shortly followed up by the 'it only needs a little help...' the alarms should start shrieking.

That 'help' is likely to cost you thousands of dollars and when that book sells 30 copies in the first year (20 were purchased by family and friends), you know what that enthusiastic publisher is going to tell you? Yep, you're right. *I guess readers just didn't like your book.*

A good part of that viral-path success comes from getting your book in front of readers. That means it really has to engage readers and companies who are only interested in your money do not spend that editing money you give them on quality work. That is, as I said, expensive. No, they pay someone minimum wage to fix typos, obvious grammar errors, and punctuation. The prose quality is not improved – not in any of the books I've looked at from these publishers. Then you need effective promotion. Notice that word 'effective'?

Promoting your book effectively – yes, we'll get to the how-to shortly – is time consuming and it requires you to keep an eye on trends in the marketplace. They change. Rapidly. If you were to hire someone to do an effective job of promoting your book, you'd have to spend a lot of money if that person offering the service was to make a decent hourly wage. The scam publishers don't promote their books. They slap them up on their website and plunk them into the online bookstores. And guess what? While readers initially don't care who publishes a book, if they buy a couple of titles from Publisher A and the books are absolutely awful, they won't buy any more books published by Publisher A. The scammers publish everybody, even though they will claim to be selective. Legitimate small-press publishers *are* selective. They want readers to feel confident that if this book has been published by this publisher, it'll be a good quality read. It won't be full of typos or be a rambling monologue that might have been written by a sixth-grader. (No, I'm not exaggerating, folk. I found all these examples and more among my random purchases from some of the scam publishers).

How do you evaluate the quality of a publisher? Read a couple of random books – not the top sellers promoted by the company. You want to see what they usually publish. Yes, you're going to drop a few bucks for a couple or three print books or some ebooks, but you may end up spending a big bunch of bucks with this company. That initial $25 investment could turn out to be very very worthwhile if it keeps you from spending $3000 with a company that produces a poor quality book, even though they're charging premium prices for editing and production services. It's very important to do this if you plan on having the publisher produce your book in print. A poor quality job does not endear you to readers. I received a new book in the mail from one of these publishers and the pages fell loose from the cover as soon as I cracked it open. Look at the quality of the printing, the paper, the cover. Is this what you want for your beloved book?

Rights! Rights! Rights! What exactly do you own?

Not everybody is going to publish their own work. Many of you will decide...and *should* decide...that the desk job makes much more sense for you than starting your own business. You're going to be looking for a small press publisher to do the work for you, leaving you to deal with only the promotional work. Yes, folk, you are going to have to promote your own book if you want to grow significant sales. The publisher is going to promote the entire catalog of published work, but you need to promote *your* book. More on that later, as I've promised.

When you allow someone to publish your book, you are granting that person or company a license to use your words. You own those words. The moment you write them down on paper or hit 'save' on your computer and save them to your hard drive, they are protected by US copyright law and you own that copyright. You can register that work with the US copyright office, but it is not necessary. It is an extra level of defense if you think there's a significant likelihood that someone will attempt to pirate your work. By all means visit the US Copyright Office's website and educate yourself. It costs $35 dollars to register your copyright online and you can upload your book directly to the archives as a digital file. It is easy to pirate digital work, so that extra step of registering your copyright adds peace of mind for a very small fee.

Once your book is finished, you, as the author, own the copyright. You can keep that copyright and allow other people to use that copyright – that book – in limited ways. Or, you can sell that copyright entirely. If you do that, you can never use those specific words and characters and scenes again without legal permission from the new owner of the copyright.

Let's translate this into plain English, shall we?

Once your book is finished, nobody can publish that book or print out part or all of it and use it on their website, as part of their own book, or in any other manner without your permission. There is a 'fair use' statute that does allow them to, say, print out a chapter as an example of good dialogue for their writing class without violating your copyright (and be glad that this teacher is giving you free promotion). But someone cannot include that same scene in the book they plan to publish on writing without getting your permission to include it. They're going to make money from that book, they're going to make money from your words. They need your permission or they need to pay your for that use. (Personally, I'd be happy to see my name put in front of those readers and wouldn't ask for pay.)

And, ahem, if you want to include a chunk of someone else's words in your book that you plan to publish and sell, yes, you do need to get permission. And that includes words published on a blog or website, too. Everything you write is protected by copyright, whether it's on your webpage, in an ebook, or on the printed page. So ask, before you include that nice example from somebody's blog in your own blog or that book you're going to publish. Nearly everybody is happy to see someone else do a bit of free promotion for them!

So what about the publisher of your book?

You are going to give the publisher the right to reproduce your words and sell them. You will get a cut, the publisher will get a cut, but you want to continue to own those words. You need to sign a contract with any publisher. ANY publisher. The contract spells out in writing how you will allow that publisher to use your words and what that publisher is not allowed to do. You are going to grant that publisher certain rights and you want to make sure that certain safeguards are built into the contract so that you keep control of your words.

First Rights: Most publishers want First Rights. That means this publisher gets to publish these words for the very first time, anywhere. They can be limited, such as First North American rights, meaning that the publisher only has the right to publish in the US, Canada, and Mexico. They are usually First World Rights today. 'Second Rights' or 'Anthology Rights' grant the publisher the right to publish a work which has already been published by someone else, as long as the rights have reverted to you.

What does that mean? Let's look at 'exclusive' and 'non-exclusive' rights.

Exclusive Rights: When you see the word 'exclusive' it means that only this publisher can do this. If you grant a publisher Exclusive First World Rights you are giving the publisher the right to make the book available to readers for the first time, anywhere in the world, and nobody else can publish that book while this publisher holds that Exclusive right.

Non-exclusive Rights: This means that while you grant this publisher the right to publish your book you may also allow other publishers to publish the book at the same time.

But remember – if you have granted Non-Exclusive rights to one publisher, you cannot grant Exclusive rights to a second publisher. That second publisher expects to be the only company to produce your book for readers, remember? You can't offer that, if you have allowed someone else to publish the book, you can only offer Non-Exclusive rights.

Do you see the danger in Exclusive rights yet? What if that publisher gets depressed, isn't making money, and stops marketing your book? But that publisher has the exclusive right to publish it. Now, you cannot allow anybody else to publish the book, unless that publisher gives you back the right to do so, in writing.

Uh oh. What if that publisher disappears on a long trek of self-discovery in Africa? Your book is stuck until you can track this person down. In today's world of small, hopeful start-up publishers, this can happen, folks! Or what if you didn't do your homework and the book is very poorly produced? Readers make negative comments about it on well-read blogs, and you'd love to pull it and republish it with a better company.

Too bad. They hold the exclusive right to publish it.

Always make sure that you have an 'escape hatch' when you sign that contract. You and the publisher need to agree on a length of time that this publisher can hold that exclusive right. Most publishers specify a set time period of time for the contractual agreement. You might both have the opportunity to renegotiate the contract in, say, two years from date of publication. At that time, you may choose to terminate and go elsewhere or you might choose to remain with this publisher. If the publisher goes on that voyage of self discovery, never to be heard from again, you get the rights back at the end of that two year period and can republish the book.

Other publishers simply include a clause that permits either the publisher or the author to terminate the contract at any time after a set period of time following publication (often one year) by means of a formal letter. In this case, if your publisher heads for Africa, you send a formal letter of termination to his last known address and you've got your rights back.

Make sure that you have the option to get your book back!

I have seen contracts that allow the publisher to hold those exclusive rights forever.

I have seen contracts that obligate the author to publish *all* future books set in that world or including those characters with this publisher.

I have seen contracts that grant this publisher the option to publish the next book you write, period.

Those final two contract items are not necessarily a problem if you love the publisher, but if you do not love the publisher and you've neglected to include that critical 'escape hatch' so that publisher can hold the rights forever, you have just obligated yourself to publish all your books with this publisher forever. Now that is scary!

All Right and Other Traps

So, now you understand the ins and outs of First, Second, Exclusive, and Non-exclusive rights. You own way more than that. You can assign all kinds of specific rights to a publisher; print rights, Book-club Rights, Audio-book Rights, Electronic Rights, Video or Movie Rights, Serial Rights. Each of these terms – and you see some variations on them – allows a publisher to produce your story for sale to buyers in a specific way. Book Club Rights are pretty self-explanatory, as are Audio-book Rights. Electronic Rights covers digital books – ebooks – and is a very important right to control, today.

Let's say that you have published your book with Book Publishers Northwest, and they are producing only print copies. You want to bring the book out as an ebook. An audio book publisher has approached you about turning the book into an audio book. How cool! Can you do it?

Maybe.

Look at your contract. You know that you assigned First Exclusive World Print Rights to Book Publishers Northwest. But what exactly are they exclusively allowed to do? They are exclusively allowed to publish the first print version of your book, so you're good to go! Give that ebook publisher and audio-book publisher a happy thumbs up and let them bring the book out in ebook form and as an audio book. But wait! That is often not the case. Your contract may give them the right to publish exclusively in print and all other forms, or some language to that effect. That, by the way, is the norm with contracts drawn up by the big legacy publishing houses.

Uh oh. Now you cannot publish that ebook form or the audio book form unless Book Publishers Northwest gives you written permission to do so. If they feel that audio book sales or ebook sales will cut into their bottom line, then they will say no. Do pay close attention to your electronic rights particularly. You want to bring that book out as an ebook and print book, both, most of the time. Make sure that if the print publisher you choose to work with does not publish in ebook format, that this publisher is willing to let you publish that ebook with another company or on your own. Send an email or snail mail letter and ask, so that you have the answer in writing.

Then, there are the contracts that acquire All Rights. All Rights, folks, means that you *sell this publisher your copyright.* It's gone. Over. You no longer have any control of those words, you no longer own them, you no longer have the right to use them without purchasing that right back from the publisher or getting written permission – not even on your website or advertising material. Unless you are doing Work For Hire, where you write, say, a brochure, textbook, instruction manual for a company, individual, or publisher, and expect to have no ownership of that project you are getting paid to write, you never, ever, ever, *ever* want to sell anyone All Rights to your work.

Ever.

That clear enough?

Never allow someone to publish your work without a written contract. If you do, that person may claim that you intended to sell All Rights and since there is nothing in writing to prove otherwise, it's your word against that person's word. In general, the legal system is not impressed with people who do not use contracts. No contract means that the publisher can do anything. Nothing is prohibited. The publisher can sell the movie rights for a bundle and pocket the money. First you'll find out is when that movie shows up on the screen and seems awfully familiar... Your name won't even be in the credits. Good luck proving anything. If you granted only First World Print Rights in a written contract then that publisher can't do that. That publisher can only publish your book on paper. If your contract specifically excluded Video and Movie Rights from the contract that otherwise awarded the publisher First World Rights (no 'print' limitation, they publish ebooks and audio-books, too), then they cannot make use of your video rights or sell them to someone else.

I see many bad contracts in today's exploding publishing world. Most of those, I suspect, are simply a matter of a new, inexperienced publisher who lacks any experience with contract language or law. If you are not sure what that legal language means, find a publishing attorney and get some help. You'll spend a hundred bucks or so on that legal opinion, but it can save you from making a mistake that will cost you much much more money in the long run.

Legacy Gotchas

So, am I saying that we should all turn our backs on the big New York, legacy publishers and go it alone?

No, I'm not saying that at all!

I do send clients to agents if I feel that they have a book that fits the increasingly narrow market niches of the legacy publishers. Let's face it, an awful lot of readers still go to the brick and mortar bookstores to find their next read, and only the big publishers can stock books in all the brick and mortar stores across the country. Your print book will end up on the New Release shelf and get sent for review to the big reviewers. Remember that the Legacy paradigm is exactly the opposite of the Indie paradigm. That is, while you will see your strong sales in the future with Indie – the 'long tail' effect – you will like see your strongest sales in the first six months to a year after a Legacy release. It is a way to get your book in front of a lot of readers very quickly. If your book does catch an expanding reader interest and you do go 'bestseller' you are fine. Your sales will take the viral path, and yes, maybe you'll become the next Grisham or Rowling or Nora Roberts.

But do realize that this happens very very rarely, whether you publish Indie or Legacy. It really is not likely to happen to your book, although every one of us believes that it will, of course.

What does happen, if your sales do not take off in that first year or so, is that the print edition will probably go OP, out of print. It's too expensive to print all those books if they're not selling well, and bookstores have seen their shelf space get more and more expensive every year as rent and utilities rise. So they won't stock books that are not in high demand. Used to be that once the print book was OP, if you had a decent agent who had amended your NY contract well (more on agents in a bit here), you'd get your rights back. Then you could go ahead and republish the book yourself or find a small press commercial publisher who wanted to re-publish it.

It's a little different today. Enter the ebook. When they first came on the scene, nobody had e-readers and reading books on the computer screen at home or the office really didn't appeal to most people. So the Legacy publishers weren't too tough about acquiring Electronic Rights. They were initially included in the standard publishing contract, but an aggressive agent could pry them loose and keep them for the author, along with Movie Rights, Foreign Rights, and Audio-book Rights.

Once the ebooks started to take off, that ended. You cannot keep your Electronic Rights if you publish with the Legacies, unless you are already a best-selling Indie author and they are dying to have you onboard. One author recent-ly negotiated just such a deal, keeping his Electronic Rights while granting one of the Big Four publishers the right to publish his book in print. And that, folks, tells you just how much power you can acquire as an Indie author with block-buster sales!

So what happens today? Today, your book that went OP in print, is probably alive and well as an ebook. Hey, it doesn't cost the publisher anything to maintain that ebook in the online bookstores. They can stick it up there, rake in whatever money it brings in, and forget it, otherwise. Is this bad? No. But you are going to earn a very very small return on each sale. As of today, 2013, the royalties on ebooks for

Legacy authors is tiny. If you publish that ebook yourself, you're going to generally earn around 1/3 of the cover price per book sold. You are going to earn far less that from the Legacy publisher. It's not the end of the world – your book is available to readers, where before, it would have been available only in the used book stores. You simply won't make as much money from those sales.

If your goal is a lifetime career as a writer, it does make more financial sense today to start out on your own and see how your story fares in today's published slush-pile. If you do moderately well – what used to be called 'mid-list' – with steady but not spectacular sales, you are going to make more money over the course of your career as an Indie author than you would make with the Legacy publishers, as things stand today. But remember – this means you are willing to start a business.

If you catch that brass ring and your book goes bestseller, believe me, the Legacy publishers are going to knock on your door. They are looking at Indie best-sellers for their next book purchase right now. You have risen out of that published slush-pile and they want you. But now, you are in a position to do a little horse-trading and get the best bargain with that publisher that you and your agent can negotiate. Now, you have something they want.

Agents, Agendas, and Attorneys

Notice that I keep mentioning agents? Agents were a big part of the old-days Legacy publishing paradigm. Most of the Legacy publishers require agented submissions only. Agents went through the slush-pile first, reading queries and looking at manuscripts to choose those few that were marketable enough to appeal to the Legacy editors. Those agents visited editors regularly, 'did lunch', and generally kept their fingers on the pulse of publishing. They knew what various editors were looking for right now and tried to supply those editors with what they needed. They earned 15% of every dime their clients made and they worked hard for those clients.

The sort of 'Hollywood' myth was the agent who became the nagging mother, the confessor, the bosom-buddy of the creative author. I never knew anybody who actually had an agent like that. Maybe that type of agent was more part of the movie and TV world. The agents I knew, like my own agent, were all business. They altered the 'boiler-plate' Legacy contracts in the author's favor, negotiated rights with the publisher, and of course, most importantly, shopped your next book to publishers to get it sold for the most money possible. And yes, my agent did and does nag me about writing the next book!

Yes, there were plenty of scams, even back then. These scam 'agencies' collected fees from the authors and 'submitted' their work to lots of publishers – charging the author for each submission. I pointed out to one naïve author that the 'agency' had submitted his mystery to several publishers who only published textbooks. And charged him fifty bucks for each of those submissions. These 'agencies' were rarely located near Manhattan, the center of Legacy publishing, and they often 'submitted' those manuscripts in large bundles, sent cheaply through the mail. They took everybody on – they were earning most of their money from the fees rather than from the success of their authors so why waste money on first-class postage or hanging out in New York? The Legacy editors all knew who these scammers were. Most of those bundles, I've heard from several Legacy editors, went straight into the recycle bin, after a cursory glance. Many did not even get out of the mail-room.

Agents are struggling today, even legitimate agents. The Legacy publishers keep contracting, reducing their lists, raising the bar on sales numbers for authors and shedding the low-sellers more aggressively. Agent earnings are falling. It's harder for them to make a living and they have to live in New York. Not a cheap city to do business in.

Alas, that has resulted in some disturbing new trends. Quite often, querying authors will get a 'this is interesting but needs some editing' response from an agent, followed by a 'I can recommend a couple of good editors for you'... Well, folks, this type of thing has been around for a long time. The author assumes that once the book is edited, of course the agent will take it and place it. So when that author learns the high cost of that editing job, he/she gulps and yanks the belt tighter. Hey, it's a lot of money, several thousand dollars, but the book is virtually sold, so....

Unfortunately, what the hopeful author does not realize is that the book is not virtually sold. The agent rather carefully made absolutely no promises about taking the book on once it was edited. (I have read a number of these letters). And guess what? That 'editor' may well be sending the agent a nice little commission for referring that client. (Shocked! I'm shocked I tell you...) That little 'thank you' is money in the agent's pocket for no work whatsoever. It's steady business for the editor buddy. And, when the book comes back to that agent, after that four or five thousand dollars worth of editing, that author may well get a nice rejection; *Gee, it's a great book, I love it, but not right for the market at the moment....* Or maybe the agent will send it to an editor or two and then shrug. Well, now you have a nicely edited book that you can publish yourself, don't you? Hopefully, the person that agent recommended to you did a good job, although you did pay premium price. And the agent is a bit richer. Hey, I told you it's getting harder and harder to make a buck as an agent these days...

If you publish with the Legacy publishers you must sign with an agent. The publishing contracts used by the big New York houses are complex, are many pages of very small print, and strongly favor the publishers. If you sign one, unaltered, you will lose a lot of money over the course of that book's career. You will discover that you have most likely signed away your movie rights, foreign rights, and all kinds of other rights. These rights can earn you money. All of my New York published SF books have been republished as foreign editions in a variety of languages. I made money from each of these re-sales and had to do no more work on the book. If my agent had not negotiated my contract for me, the publisher would have received that money, rather than me.

Do realize that agents only deal with the big Legacy publishers in New York. The small press commercial publishers have never been on their radar. The reason for that is that the agent, the legitimate agent, makes his or her money only from your financial success. My agent took 15% of my checks from the publishers, right off the top; including the initial advance and all royalties. Very very few small press commercial publishers can afford to pay an author an advance. That means the agent only earns money from your sales, and since sales through small press houses tend to see the same long-tail sales curve that Indie books do, the agent is not likely to make a lot of money for his or her time. At least not right away. Additionally, the success of the Indie or small press book is highly dependent on the viral path. If the author doesn't work hard at promoting the book, it may never achieve that viral sales curve. That leaves the ultimate success of the book out of the agent's hands. Considering the high overhead of operating in New York, most agents choose to devote their efforts to authors publishing with the Legacy houses.

We have a opened a huge niche for the publishing attorney. Many new authors really need help to evaluate the contracts offered by publishers these days. Many of those contracts are awful, not necessarily because the publisher has evil intent, but because that publisher may have no idea how to write an effective contract and the author does not know what questions to ask. And some contracts are intentionally poor. I have had clients who have been accepted by a small press publisher, only to be dropped when that client insisted on a termination clause so that the author could reclaim the book after a certain period of time, if desired. That publisher wanted permanent control of that book and was not willing to give it up.

Educate yourself on your rights. Right now, Daniel Steven, a publishing attorney who writes a column for Mystery Writers of America's newsletter, has published numerous articles on publishing rights and what you, as a new author, need to know. His work is featured on Publishlawyer.com, a good website to visit as you educate yourself;

http://www.publishlawyer.com/ You'll find numerous informative articles on contracts of all sorts on that website. In general, a publishing attorney such as Mr. Stevens will charge you a flat fee or a standard hourly rate to review that publishing contract that is confusing you. It can be difficult to wrap your head around 'larger-picture' issues, such as 'what happens to your rights if this publisher goes bankrupt'. Do be sure that you know what are you are signing and, more importantly, what needs to be included in that contract in order to ensure the safety of your rights. One of the dangers in today's volatile new publishing is bankruptcy. Many hopeful new publishers start out by funding their business on their credit card. If they don't start making money, they'll quit. What happens to that book now? Unless you are publishing the book yourself and retaining all rights to the work, you need to have a thorough understanding of your legal rights.

I've also published a handbook for new writers on contracts and copyright, through my Literary Midwife series: *Rights and Contracts; What YOU Need to Know About Copyright, Rights, ISBNs, and Contracts,* available as an ebook.

The bottom line, folks, is to educate yourself about what you own when you finish that book, and what you can and cannot expect from publishers and agents. The more you know, the better educated you are, the less likely you are to get taken by a scam or find yourself in an unfortunate legal position. It is your book. Only you can protect it

CHAPTER 7

Effective Promotion

E arlier, I suggested that the time to start promoting your book was before you were done with it. I could hear all those gasps of protest. *I don't have anything to put on a website! I don't have anything talk about on a blog! I hate Facebook! I hate blogging! It takes time away from my writing...*

Yep, I hear you. And every one of those arguments rises from your misunderstanding of what makes promotion work for you and your books, even the 'time away from my writing' one. Let's start looking at those reactions one at a time. But first, let's review that viral path once more, shall we? Your book sales will increase as happy readers tell their friends all about this new good read. But first, you have to get that book in front of the people who are going to read it and rave about it to their friends. When nobody has read you and therefore can't rave yet, what do you do?

You introduce yourself to them and help them decide that you've probably written a good book.

Nearly all new authors assume that promotion means telling readers all about the book that they're selling and their life as an author. I see so many novice-author blogs with the book thumbnail and buy link at the top of the page. Then there's the most recent blog entry. The author tells how he went for a walk on the beach and then came back to write 3 pages on Chapter Ten of the next book. Or she talks about her lunch of cottage cheese and fresh tomatoes and how her character finally told her that she didn't trust the new man in her life, so now she has to come up with a new romantic interest... They even tweet short versions of this news and/or post it on their Facebook pages.

Essentially, these authors are talking to their fans, who are just dying to know what they ate for breakfast and how the next book is coming along.

Well, that's great if you have a huge fan base that already buys all your books and you don't need to acquire new fans because your viral path has already turned into a superhighway. But you're a new author, right? You can probably count your current fans on both hands and maybe have fingers left over if you haven't published anything yet. This type of 'I'm a celebrity' writing feels great – don't we all want to be a celebrity? – and gets you nothing. And yes, these same authors whose blogs and Facebook pages I've monitored make sour public comments about how they blogged and did the Facebook page and their book sold 30 copies in the first six months. Obviously, they say, blogging and Facebook don't work as promotional tools.

Folks, you have to do it *right*.

Every PR article out there is going to tell you to blog or use social media, as if that's magic. Just start a Facebook page and the world will flock to your book!

Why should that happen when nobody knows you? How do you even get someone to come to your blog or your Facebook page, never mind buy your book? Let's look at the process.

A gazillion blogs and social media pages clutter the internet. Someone can click around forever and never land on the same page twice. And people don't do that. How do they find new sites? A friend forwards a link or a blog entry. We like to share cool finds on the internet with our friends. A few of the recipients like the post or the page and click over to that website or blog to take a look for themselves. They are entertained. They sign up for the blog or the newsletter. Now you have a new follower and potential new fan.

Here's the key: They are entertained.

Entertainment. Doesn't that sound familiar? I think I've mentioned it before a few times here, haven't I? Remember, that is what we are all selling, whether we've published a memoir, a book on Sicilian cooking, a mystery, a thriller, or a romance. Write that word on a sticky note if you haven't already done so, and stick it onto your monitor.

Let's start with the basics: What are your readers buying when they buy your book? If it's a fiction book, they're buying an 'escape' of some sort – an adventure, thrills, romance. If they're a non-fiction reader, they're buying information. In both cases, the bottom line is that they're buying entertainment. Even the nonfiction reader who wants to learn something from your book wants to enjoy the experience.

Entertainment is the key to effective promotion. How? Remember that today's burning issue is 'how do you find your next read'. Most readers either buy the next book of a favorite author, they hear about a great new book from a friend, or they read a great review on a review site they visit regularly and trust. Or, of course, they visit the New Release shelf in the bookstore. But unless you're publishing with the Legacy publishers, your book likely won't be there. And if you are publishing with the Legacy publishers, it won't be there for long.

If you don't yet have a book out, the 'review' and 'hear from a friend' options aren't available to you, are they? But we're talking entertainment, remember? That covers a lot more ground than just this book. There are a lot of ways to entertain potential fans. If you entertain them on your website and blog, if they find you articulate, witty, you post links to videos that they enjoy, your blog posts are interesting and informative about subjects that engage them and you're writing this interesting book, well, by the time you're ready to launch that book you are an 'old friend' and those blog and website regulars whom you have entertained buy your book. Why not? They like what they're reading on the website and blog. You have entertained them. They figure they'll like what they'll read in the book, too. They believe that you will entertain them some more. And, as I said, you're a friend now. Of course they'll at least give this book a try!

There is nothing more satisfying than good sales figures in the first month that the book is out! Additionally, that pre-release fan base can really work for you if you're shopping your book to agents for the Legacy publishers. The agents I've talked to say that they Google an author when they consider a manuscript. So do editors, if they're looking at submissions from authors directly. If that person has an active internet presence, a lot of activity on his or her blog, that editor or agent is much more likely to take that author on than if they come up with nothing or a blah, rarely-updated blog and website. Today more than ever, you want to bring a fan base to the bargaining table when you shop your book, especially if intend to shop it to the Legacy publishers. Notice that many authors recently published through the New York houses have public careers? They already have fans who will for sure buy at least this book, just to see if that person is a good writer. If you already have an internet fan base, you are ahead of the unpublished author who does not.

Entertaining Your Readers

I can hear you asking: How do I entertain my readers? Aha, good question! Let me counter that with a question of my own that you must answer first: Who are your readers?

What's that? Silence? I bet you haven't really thought about that, have you? Or your immediate answer is 'people who like my book'! Yes, that's true, but who are they *before* they like your book? Who are the people who are likely to enjoy your book? And most importantly...what are they likely to be interested in besides your book?

See where this is going yet?

May I direct your attention to that sticky note on your monitor? *Entertainment.*

Create an author Facebook page that is separate from your personal page. If you want to create separate pages for each book go for it, but if you do, link them back to your author page. You are going to work at letting readers know that you are entertaining, no matter what you write. Keep in touch with loved ones on your personal page and entertain strangers (who will hopefully become fans) on your author page. Entertain with the blog and back it up with a website that promotes you as an entertaining author. And now we're back to that pesky question; who are your readers?

You have to know what your readers want before you can entertain them. It's not about you, Mr. or Ms. New Author. That blog, website, social media page is all about your readers. And very few authors analyze 'readers' or give much thought to the people who like their book. Let's do it right now.

What do you write? Fantasy? Thriller? A memoir? Romance? Will it appeal more to women or men? What else is part of your world? What does your main character do? Are animals involved? A sport? Interesting foods? An unusual setting? Other activities? Religion?

One client of mine is a retired firefighter and is marketing a thriller. His main characters are father and sons, firefighters in a small town who come up against an international terrorist plot. Good thriller plot, lots of action, high stakes, some great fire scenes and action set in Iran. Who are his readers? They're probably men more than women, although the book will appeal to plenty of women as well. It's not totally male-centric, the way romances tend to be female-centric. Readers who enjoy it may be interested in outdoor activities, sports, they may be firefighters or have family members who are firefighters. They may be interested in politics, the military, the situation in the Middle East. They like action, adventure, drama.

I encouraged him to set up a website and start a blog. My client hikes and canoes a lot, and I urged him to include pictures of fires he had worked, pictures from his camping and canoe trips and to blog about those trips and his fire experiences with an emphasis on the dramatic rather than the poetic and lyrical. I encouraged him to add links to news stories that relate to the fictional events in his book, include pictures of ships like those that feature in his story, and pictures of Tehran streets where his action scenes might have taken place. I encouraged him to post 'backstory' about his characters on the website, including images, if he finds pictures of people he wants to 'cast' as his characters. (Remember that images on the internet are copyrighted, so ask before you use! Or use for-pay photo sites such as Istock or Dreamstime and purchase images for a few bucks). I encouraged him to relate the news stories to the events in his novel, to call attention to that novel regularly as he posts on his blog.

These are all methods of entertaining people who visit the blog as well as advertising the forthcoming book. Not every person will be entertained by every post on his blog, every page on his website, but some visitors will come back, since he posts regularly. They'll keep visiting. And an agent who visits will notice.

In fact, my client did indeed get at least one query about his book from an agent who had read his blog and his description of the novel-in-progress. Yes, agents and publishers do look at sites, folks. More importantly, he is building a readership. When the book is finally published, no matter who publishes it, he already has fans who want to read it.

Think about your future readers. Make a list of everything they might be interested in, starting with topics that relate to your book. Another client of mine is writing a romantic suspense book set is a picturesque little town on the Northern California coast. Her readers are likely women more than men, mystery lovers, women who are probably romance readers as well. She can include pictures and details about the real town, describing how she fictionalized this or that business or location to suit the book, or why she set a particular scene here. She can include travel information about interesting things to do in the area, places to stay, good restaurants. I found that quite a few of my mystery readers actually visited places mentioned in my books when they traveled in the area where the stories took place. She might include recipes for dishes mentioned in the book, gardening tips, activities for kids (the protagonist is a recently-widowed mother with two children), and so on. She might talk about how she wondered if she was encountering a ghost on a late night stroll (a ghost features in the suspense plot). Maybe she'll upload a video of a quick walking tour of the house where the story is set. Readers may share the travel tips, the lovely photos of the coast or the quaint, Victorian seaside homes, the local flower show, display garden, what have you. They might share the recipes, or the posts about meeting a 'ghost' one night. That YouTube video of the town tour may get quite a few hits as people look for vacation destinations. Each time someone shares that post or link with a friend or a group of friends, the author's name and her book are introduced to new potential readers.

Look your own list over. Get creative! Don't think of this as drudgery, it doesn't have to be. You are celebrating your book, you are saying to your fans 'look at all the cool stuff I used to put this book together', and you're making new fan-friends! Find great You Tube videos that relate to your book and post links to them. Take a little digital video camera with you on your next hike or video the setting for a scene in your book, if it's set in the real world. Smart-phones take videos and some small handheld video cameras retail for well under a hundred bucks. While neither provides commercial quality videos, they do provide entertainment.

Making It In The Movies

YouTube is fertile promotional ground. An author and speech-coach cousin of mine, developing his own business, put one of these inexpensive little cameras in a water-tight plastic sphere and let it tumble down a mountain stream. It didn't relate to what he was doing with his business, specifically, but a lot of people on YouTube clicked over to his website after they viewed it. A local inspirational speaker flew her ultra-light across the country and blogged about the trip, posting pictures all the way. It netted her a huge following by the end of the trip. My client's weekend visit to the seaside town where her romantic suspense novel is set may not engage as many viewers as an ultra-light flight across the country, but a video tour of the town, posted on YouTube is certainly going to send some new potential readers to her site. Or maybe she'll video the local Fourth of July parade, full of kids, pets, and home-made floats. One benefit to those video tours...you don't have to look at yourself on the screen. If you have crippling stage fright, stay behind the camera.

If you have that hankering to be a movie star, by all means go for it! Set up a tripod or get someone to help you video yourself. Another inspirational writer did that, getting a friend to video her as she strolled with her horse in a meadow or worked in the garden and talked. Read the first few pages of your book, if it starts with a bang, or read the blurb and chat with the viewers for a few minutes about writing the book. Practice with lights and effects to make it dramatic, practice that public-reading voice. Most YouTube viewers click away after two minutes, so put out a short 'teaser' or two at first. If you find you are getting a lot of interest, then go with a longer reading and conversation, but realize that, as with the 'all about me' blog, that longer version is going to appeal mainly to people who have decided they are a fan. Use the short 'teasers' to snag the interest of YouTube browsers and send them to your site. Offer writing tips. Again, keep it short; two minutes.

Reviews and Paid Reviews

I've mentioned review sites. They may well take the place of the New Release shelf in the local bookstore in today's publishing world. There are hundreds of review sites and their value lies entirely in how many readers visit them and how often they take the recommendations of the reviewers. One of the unfortunate scams in today's publishing world is the promoter who promises to get the book reviewed on a number of sites for a hefty fee. The naïve new author who has no idea how to find review sites is assured that this will bring the book to the attention of millions of readers...

Maybe.

If those sites get millions of visits from readers who also tend to read what the reviewers recommend, then we have the 'Oprah Winfrey of the internet' and a positive review there would be worth gold. But what the naïve new author overlooks is that 'any' review site is not necessarily a *good* review site. It might get a total of ten visits from readers in a month. Or fewer. But the 'promoter' charges that nice fat fee to get the book posted there. The author is discouraged when that expensive promotional package fails to bring him or her a flood of sales. Know what the 'promoter's' answer will be? Yep. *I guess readers just didn't like your book...* That covers a lot, doesn't it? There is no 'magic' to finding review sites. Google is your friend, remember? Get online and search 'book review sites'. Start browsing. Start educating yourself. Visit those sites. Web-based sites will do more for you than print-media reviewers since most reviews will include a link to the book or the author's website or blog, and readers can quickly click over to learn more. Find out how the review sites accept submissions and submit your book.

You're a reader, right? And as an author, you are a more educated reader than many of your reader-peers, in that you can be more specific about why you do or do not think that a book is good. By all means, submit reviews to these sites. If readers find you articulate and they share your opinions about the books you review, you have endeared yourself to them with that review and you have entertained them. Keep that important E-word in mind as you write the review. Make it witty as well as informative. Entertain! That's your new mantra, remember? Entertain, entertain, entertain! Of course, the link to your website or blog should be part of your by-line on the review. Reviews – good reviews – are an excellent way to meet new readers. It can be worth it to you to write reviews for no pay if it gets your name and website link in front of lots of new potential fans.

Apart from the 'promoter' who will charge you to promote your book through review sites, some of the larger reviewers, even the Legacy reviewers, are offering 'paid reviews'. The author pays the reviewer to review the book. Do you want to do this? It certainly is not cheap, but it does put your book in front of the large readership of these Legacy-era top review platforms.

The jury is still out, as far as I am concerned at the time I write this, on whether paid reviews on the big review platforms are cost effective. I haven't received enough feedback from authors who paid for reviews to make an objective evaluation. A lot of readers do read these reviews and certainly publishers read them. But quite a few readers whose blogs I follow or whom I've talked to have been skeptical about the validity of those paid reviews. I mean, the reviewer is getting a check from the author. Isn't that a conflict of interest? So those positive reviews may not, after all, work for you as well as they should. Keep in mind that today, a good review only goes so far with Legacy publishers. It's all about sales. A really smashing sales record for your new ebook is going to be more valuable than a glowing review in *Kirkus* or *New York Times Review of Books*, whether you paid for it or not. My own opinion is that your promotional time and money are better spent on a good website and entertaining blog and a proactive promotional campaign than that one or three expensive paid reviews. I chuckled at a recent whine by a literary author who published his book and then felt that self-publishing was a loser's game when he didn't sell 50,000 copies in the first six months. His whine included the information that he had taken out paid ads in the big review magazines. Maybe they would have helped him in the long run if he had stayed the course and accepted that 'long tail' career path of the Indie author, but they certainly didn't result in an instant rush to purchase his book.

Folks, the reality is that time is more important than cash in today's publishing world. *You cannot buy the effective promotional services you need.* It's not about sticking your book cover all over the internet, it's about selling *you*, the author. What, you say? You don't have time to do this? Tch tch. We did talk about this way back at the start of this book, remember? That first chapter was all about starting a business versus taking the nine-to-five job. But even if you publish with a small press commercial publisher, if you don't have the time to promote your work, your only hope for big sales is to grab the brass ring of the best-seller, and considering how few readers are likely to be exposed to your book without at least a basic promotional platform, your chances of grabbing that brass ring are not real real high. I know this is a tough message to hear, but alas, a whole crowd of people who leaped into self-publishing never heard it, and because of that, they ended up feeling as if they had failed as writers, and that the new publishing paradigm had failed them.

Nope. They did not fail. Their books might eventually have found plenty of readers, had they persisted. They simply failed to understand *how* to succeed.

Speaking In Tongues; The Personal Author Voice

You're going to be putting a lot of words up on your blog and other peoples' blogs if you do your promotional homework. So, let's stop right here and talk about Author Voice. Some of you are lucky enough to have a strong personal voice when you write this type of narrative. Your word and grammar choices create a conversational style that will come across to the readers as a real person talking, perhaps across the kitchen table over tea, or over a beer at the local watering-hole. That creates a strong sense that you are in a one-on-one conversation with the reader, you are a friend, you are talking to me.

That is the personal connection you really want to make.

I am talking to you, friend, I am giving you my full attention.

Alas, the majority of authors who write narrative for their blog or website go all formal or literary. We're rather a self-conscious bunch when we get up on that clearly-public stage and we tend to start reaching for that poetic turn of phrase or just the right combination of Big Words to really show off our Literary Skills. Well, folks, what are your goals here? To entertain, you say? Oh, good, you've been paying attention! That is your primary intent! But you have a strong secondary intent; make a personal connection to your potential readers.

Why does that matter? Because we do things for our friends. If I like you personally and I know you're trying to build your career, well, maybe romantic suspense is not my literary cup of tea, but hey, I'll download that $3.99 ebook and give it a read just to see how well you write. And if I like it, hey, you're my friend, I'll tell everybody on my blog and

Facebook page all about this cool new romantic suspense author who is just getting started.

We are nice to our friends!

You become 'friends' with your blog readers when you talk as if you are sitting with that cup of tea or that beer, chatting after work. When you use that formal or literary style, you either sound like a college lecturer and we find ourselves sitting in a vast auditorium back in English Literature 101, or you come across as a snooty author looking down on the mere-mortal readers from your lofty and unreachable platform.

Neither of these attitudes is endearing to your readers and neither of them prompts that reader to do nice things for you because you are a friend. You clearly don't need our help!

If you are one of those people who simply have to write in a flat, descriptive style, rather like a text-book or encyclopedia entry, that's fine. Write your post that way. Get the thing down on the screen or on paper. And then revise it. What ever made you think you could only write one draft of a blog post? I certainly hope you revised your book a few times before you published it! If you talk in this dry, formal style, if this is your conversational voice, change it! Changing your voice on the page is no more difficult than changing from first to third person POV in a story or using present tense instead of past tense. Think of a friend who has a flamboyant and entertaining conversational style – you know, the person everybody loves to listen to at parties or gatherings. Now, go over your blog post and imagine that person saying these same sentences. Visualize it. Hear the tone of voice. Adopt that voice for now. Use that person's word choices, his or her style of speaking, the idiosyncratic grammar. Conversation is rarely grammatically correct! Get over it!

You're acting here, creating this Author Persona who is more entertaining than you might be in conversational real life. Hey, this is not a dating service, where you are supposed to reveal the Real You! You're here to entertain, remember? What you will find is that you will assimilate and evolve that voice until you realize one day that you now have your own Author Voice and you fall into it naturally as you sit down to write a post. I have that Author Voice. I have a palette of Voices that I use where appropriate. You need no more than one Author Voice, but do work at developing it, unless it has come 'built in'.

Why does this matter? Because people are short of time. Every day. If readers can only read a few of the blogs they've subscribed to, today, they'll read the ones that entertain first, rather than the ones that inform but are not entertaining.

Repeat after me: *Entertain, entertain, entertain!*

Reach Out; Expanding Your Blogosphere

Okay, you've polished that knock-em-dead Author Voice and you're posting lots of fun, entertaining stuff on your blog. You're blogging regularly, keeping it fresh. And your readership is growing. Slowly. Sure, people are spreading the word, reposting your posts, but the early stages of a viral path are slow. How do you speed it up?

Reach out and bring more readers to your blog.

Easy to say, eh? Oh, I hear you. *Just how do we do that, smart-girl?* You find other readers who might like your book. Where will you find them in quantity? On the blogs of other authors whose books are similar to yours.

Is this 'poaching'?

Of course not. No one author can satisfy the reading needs of your average book reader for a year. There's room for a lot of us to share our readers. Let's say that you write classical Sword-and-Sorcery fantasy. Browse the online bookstores and find authors who are writing books in that sub-genre. Go to their websites, find their blogs. Skim over them. Do they post regularly? Are they getting reader comments? Most importantly, do you like the person? Are you entertained? Can you comment on what they are posting?

Yes, this takes time. We'll talk about budgeting time in my final section of the book, where I talk about how to make all this work in your real world, especially if you have a family and/or day job. But for now, set aside a small block of time regularly and scan the blogosphere for blogs that you might enjoy visiting. Wait for a post that you think your blog readers would like to read. Contact that blog author, ask to use his or her post, and offer to link back to the blog and the author's website. Almost every blogger will give you permission to repost. Hey, this means new potential readers for that author, too! But DO ask. Those blog posts...your blog posts...are copyright protected, remember? And it's respectful. You want to build good relationships among your peers!

Post that author's blog post on your blog. Include a picture of that author if you can – you'll usually find a nice thumbnail of the author on the website or the blog's 'about the author' page. Be generous with your back-links to that author's site, books for sale page, blog, whatever. Comment on the post and why you thought your blog readers would enjoy it. Now send the link to that blog post to the author. Chances are that this author will now send his or her readers to your blog to read the positive comments you included with that re-post. And those readers – who like the same sort of books – are now introduced to you and your books. Your readers have been introduced to this author's books.

It's a win-win for both of you. And it's a win for the readers who have now discovered a new author.

We're all in this together, folks, and there's a big pool of readers out there. We can help each other out.

For more bang for your blogging buck, invite an author who writes an entertaining and active blog and publishes books that are similar to yours to be a guest on your blog for a week. Work to make it a positive experience for all. Come up with questions beforehand so that you can keep the blog conversation active, even if no readers chime in with comments or questions. There is nothing more discouraging than having your guest post one comment and get no responses, so that the blog sits inactive for the rest of that guest's time there. Don't let that happen. Ask yourself what your readers might be interested in learning and ask those questions even if your usual readers all seem to have lost their voices. Remember that people read your blog who never post. Very few blog readers post.

Ask that author if you can be a guest on his or her site in return. Usually you'll get a yes. These guest-blogger stints allow each of you to spend time entertaining new potential readers. Again, it's a win-win for everybody; authors and readers alike.

What you do not want to do is to drop in one time to the blog of an author whose books are similar to yours and make a comment that is nothing more than a blatant pitch for your own book or blog. *Gee, that was a clever comment Ms. Author, and I bet your readers would like My Great Book at www.mywebsite.com.* Ms. Author is to be totally excused if she instantly deletes that comment, and even if she does not, you are not presenting yourself well to these new potential readers. You come across as a bit of a jerk and you're not entertaining anybody. Don't do this.

The Review and Reader Sites

We're going to see more and more review sites, and many of them will be what I call 'reader sites' where the reviews are made by readers rather than by a few specified reviewers. *Goodreads* followed this model, allowing readers to post reviews and comments as they read books, and serving as a great place for readers to find their next read from the recommendations of others. Alas, *Goodreads* has been purchased by Amazon.com so we'll have to wait and see if that open marketplace model changes, but other sites based on the *Goodreads* model are springing up; *Library Thing* is gaining popularity. This is a market niche that needs to be filled and entrepreneurs will fill it.

These are sites where you want to post as a reader first, author second. Readers tend to frown on authors who contribute little to the overall conversation about books and, instead, show up to simply and obviously pitch their own work.

124 • MARY ROSENBLUM

Again, it's entertainment first, remember? You need to pay your dues and entertain with your own reviews and comments before you suggest that these readers might like your book. Coming across as a jerk who barges in to post a sales pitch is not a way to endear yourself to readers. Most readers, myself included, would rather read a book written by an author who seems like a nice person and joins the party rather than someone whose only concern is to Sell My Books.

But you are a reader as well as a writer, right? Contribute to these review sites, as I mentioned before. Remember – you are an author, so you can be more specific than a lot of folk when you post feedback on books.

One word here, people. When you review the work of others, do not do it in a negative manner. Ever. Ever. Ever. Not only does that, once again, make you seem like a jerk, but how would you like it? You wouldn't, huh? Then don't do it. If you hate the book, ignore it. Review something you did enjoy. If you see a post that sings a book's praises to the sky when you thought it was poorly written, and you suspect the poster is the brother of the author, then by all means jump in with a bit of gentle disagreement – you want to keep these review sites trustworthy – but do it politely. *I agree that Mygreatbook had some super description in it. I have to say, though, that I found the plot very slow. I didn't get past Chapter Seventeen. Maybe, in his next book, Mr. Author will leave out all those details about how everything was done.*

Now you've added a gentle balance to the hyperbolic *this is a masterpiece* post left by the author's brother, but you have done it in a constructive and positive fashion, mentioning what the author did well before disagreeing specifically with that 'masterpiece' review.

Enter Stage Right; There Is No Exit!

Remember that anything you post on the internet persists. If you throw a temper tantrum or come across as a jerk, it's going to hurt you with future potential readers, long, long after you have gotten over your annoyance. Remember that potential fans who haven't read any of your books may go buy one and try it if they find you articulate and interesting on your blog, your website, or on other public forums where you have posted.

You are on stage, 24/7.

Daunting, huh? Well, it kind of is. Keep it in mind that you are a public figure now. As an Author, your books will be judged by how you behave, how you write online, and your attitude toward others. This is why I suggested earlier in this section that you create a Facebook page that is only available to the family and friends that you can relax and be yourself in front of. That doesn't stop them from plastering an unfortunate quote all over their own media space if you vent about something, but it's not as damaging as acting like a jerk directly in front of your fans.

Think first and edit, before you post on your Author site. Always. ALWAYS. Your blog or social media posts as Author are not a conversation after work at the local watering hole, even if you strive to give your posts that casual and intimate feel. You are a walking promotion for your book. Don't like that idea? Hey, be yourself and take the consequences. They won't be bad if you're not a native jerk, but if you are, yeah, you'll lose some potential readers who won't try your books because they don't like your attitude. But you know what? If you grab that brass ring and go best-seller, they'll probably buy your book anyway. It's simply better, in terms of finding that viral path on your own, if you come across as someone who is articulate, entertaining, (ah, the e-word again!) and a Nice Person.

If something rouses your emotions, write out the post as a word processor file, save it, and post it tomorrow, after you have calmed down and reread it. It can be easy to forget that many thousands of people may read that nasty comment you tossed off in a fit of anger. Save that comment for a cooler moment and an editorial eye.

The bottom line is always that you are promoting yourself and your books. You are not at a party among dear friends who will accept bad behavior on your part.

Get feedback on your blog posts from experts in the blogging field if you can – people who know what a good Author blog is and how to improve one. The copyblogger universe is full of instructors, high-priced workshops, and books on how to write good copy and increase your blog traffic. Their pitch and style tend to be different than the style that works best for authors - but they have the 'learn how to do it well' thing down. We need that in our field, too. Learn how to blog well, it will pay off in the end! And remember, every word you post on the internet is either helping or hurting your sales and your career as Author. Do your best to make them help you!

The Social Media Quagmire

Social media sites abound, from the 1000--pound gorilla of Facebook to the new sites gaining prominence such as

Pinterest, Wattpad, Tumbler, Scribn, and a host of others yet to come. These sites all offer similar options; get the link to your website/blog/books in front of new people. That is your goal here; entertain and entice new potential fans to your books. The downside is that this is a huge bog. Oh, it's lovely all right, verdant, dotted with colorful orchids and little puddles that reflect the blue summer sky... And then you wander in.

And sink into quicksand.

The social media sites are a great place to totally squander your writing time, folks. YouTube is probably an even better time-sink, but you can at least tell yourself you're being productive as you keep up with Faccbook, Pinterest, Tumbler, and check your Wattpad and Scribn chapters to see how many hits they got. New sites crop up and get popular and your writing-time dollar gets stretched thinner and thinner or gets spent wholly on these 'promotional' activities. We'll talk about that critical time budget in the next section, don't worry.

The key to using social media sites is to use them effectively. There's another e-word to stick up on your monitor; effectively. If you're going to spend your valuable writing hours on that social media site, make sure you're picking up potential new fans there. Think about what that site does best and decide if you are going to generate enough interest there to make that time expenditure worthwhile. Let's look at Pinterest. As I write this, Pinterest has taken off. It's a sharing site where people post images mostly, that can be 're-pinned' to collages, 'boards', put together by Pinterest members. The images can circulate endlessly to various boards and the link to your website or blog is attached. It's a hot site right now and a lot of people follow individuals, just as they follow people on Facebook. So should you jump in there?

Maybe. Maybe not. Let's look at whether it will work for you and your books. Let's say you're working on a YA fantasy series and you're an artist. You've entertained yourself by painting dozens of water colors featuring your characters in various scenes from the novel. You've Photoshopped fabulous scenes and collages to illustrate the book. Or, you've taken lots of photos of places where the action in your mystery will take place. Since it's set on the northern California coast, those pictures of beach, rocky coastline, and quaint Victorian summer homes from a bygone era are pretty nice, as are the sweeping vistas of vineyards. You start posting these images on Pinterest and yes, people start pinning them. Those people who use them notice that this is a scene from your book and those who are YA fans or mystery fans might even click over to your blog or website and take a look. Some of them will actually buy something. Some of those new readers will absolutely love the book and rave about it all over the place. Bingo. A few more steps gained on the viral-path!

So here, your skills with Photoshop, your camera, or a paintbrush, are all desirable commodities on this site. One author client of mine makes fabulous masks. Photos of those masks, especially the ones representing characters from her children's book, would be a wonderful Pinterest upload. Yes, it's probably worth spending time here. But what if you are a total klutz with a camera, can't work those pesky graphics programs, and have the artistic talents of a cantaloupe? Well, you can upload the cover that someone made for you, you can pin together interesting boards with other peoples' images and make some kind of connection to your book, but probably, you're better off spending your time on a different site.

Your writing time is a finite quantity and you want to spend it wisely. We'll get to a careful look at that issue, in our final section of the book.

Giving It Away

Book sharing sites have proved to be an effective way of bringing in new readers. These are sites like Wattpad, a Canadian site frequented by a lot of YA readers, and Scribn, a site that is more adult oriented. Authors post content for readers to read, comment on, and recommend. I can hear you right now; Give my book away? You've got to be kidding! And someone might steal it!

Well, your work is still copyrighted to you, even though you upload it somewhere for people to read for free, and even well published work with a registered copyright gets pirated. We'll talk about dealing with piracy issues later on, as well. Let's review that viral path yet again. The more people who rave about your book to their friends, the more readers you will acquire. One way to boost that initially-slow progression from One Reader to Many Many Readers is to get lots of people to read the book right off. Putting your book out as an ebook that is free for the first month is one effective way to get the viral-path ball rolling a bit faster than it might otherwise. A client of mine sold more than 1000 copies of her YA ebook in the first month, after putting the book out for free, initially. Those 1000 sales resulted from the readers of the free book telling their friends about it. Selling 1000 books in the first month as a brand new author without any name recognition is pretty good.

Putting the book out on Wattpad has a similar effect. Yes, it's up there forever, but if readers on Wattpad love it and tell their friends, most of them will probably sample it and if they like it, they'll buy your ebook or the print version. Most people prefer to read an ebook on a reader rather than a website screen or they like paper. You lose some sales, sure, but you gain a wider distribution of your book to people who have never heard of you and might not stumble across your blog or webpage. Several authors have taken the path of uploading the book to the book-sharing sites one chapter at a time. The book has already been published and the buy-link is available on the sharing-site of course. Many authors have seen immediate and significant increases in their book sales as readers got several chapters into the story and decided that they liked it and wanted to read the entire book right now, rather than wait for the chapters, or open one chapter at a time on the website.

If you are possessive about your work and your attitude is that 'nobody gets a word from me unless they pay for it', you are casting aside a valuable promotional tool. This is why stores offer 'loss leaders'. Those items on sale may not net them much or any profit, but the other things that people buy while they're in the store and the new customers they acquire more than make up for the loss of profit on the sale items. You may not make any money on the free ebook collection of your short stories that you give away when someone signs up for your newsletter, but if you create a fan who buys the next five books and raves about them to everybody, you're well ahead on the viral path.

I recommend to my clients who write short fiction as well as novel length work that if their short fiction does not sell to the top markets, instead of continuing to try and place it in the ezines that don't pay, make it available as a 99 cent ebook – longer stories and mini-collections of shorter stories are popular in this form – post it on your website as a free read, or give it away as a downloadable pdf to anyone who signs up on your mailing list. That email list is the coin of this internet realm and a way to announce your next book or a sale to your fans.

Creative Pricing

Play with your prices. Amazon.com allows for flexible pricing so that you can put books on sale or even give ebooks away for free. That, however, may be affected by how you get your book onto Amazon.com – if you publish your ebook through their portal, you may not be able to reduce the price to free, where you can if you are published by an aggregator like Smashwords and the book Is then distributed to Amazon.com. You will most likely not be able to give away a print-on-demand paper book for free unless you are willing to cover the production cost out of pocket yourself – potentially a very spendy promotion! But you may be able to reduce the cover price for a sale so that you make no money on the book, but the very attractive price brings you new readers.

Sales and giveaways are a great way to spur plateauing sales. And remember – you are swapping dollar profits now, for readers who will buy your books later. Think of those sales as an investment. You are plowing that money you didn't earn back into your brand by using it to bring you more readers who will buy your work in the future. Many authors reduce the price of early books in a series, simply to encourage readers to get started. Those that love the series will pay the higher price for later books. Use a tracking system such as Google Analytics and experiment with sales and giveaways. Try giving that book away for free for a week, or mark something down to 99 cents for a month. Most internet bookselling sites will accommodate sales like that, although print book pricing is less flexible since you have to cover the cost of producing that print book.

I do not recommend putting your one and only book out as a free ebook, unless it is a 'prelaunch sale' for a limited time. For awhile, new authors would put the first book out for free to 'build a readership' and count on selling the second book. Quite a few of those books were very poorly written and that 'free' price-tag, when it was not a sale price, quickly came to mean 'lousy author trying to find readers'. It is certainly worth pricing your first book as a new author well below the prices that the Legacy books are getting. You are a nobody to those new readers and you're asking them to plunk down their hard earned cash and take a chance that you actually know how to write a good story. Remember that we're publishing the slush pile! There are a lot of books out there that are, shall we say, of less than top quality. You want your price to reflect your confidence that the book is worth money, but on the other hand, you want that interested reader with a lean wallet to toss down that cash and take a chance.

This is where ebooks come in as an outstanding promotional tool. You can put your early books out cheaply and price them at, say, $3.99. That's not a lot of cash to spend if the cover and blurb are enticing and a brief read inside – and just about all buyers do that – has convinced them that you can at least put sentences together well. By all means back that ebook up with a print version as well. You can do that later on, after you've established a fan base, or from the start. Many people who read a book electronically first time, will buy the print copy. Most readers still prefer print to screen for reading and they like a well stocked bookshelf. That Is certainly changing, but it's true at this moment.

The price for ebooks is slowly rising. Do some browsing on the internet and see what the Legacy publishers are charging. Monitor the ebook best-seller lists and notice what the non-Legacy published ebooks in the top 25 lists are selling for. Usually, they are priced significantly less than the Legacy-published ebooks. Pay attention to the royalty paid you by the online bookstores. Usually, the royalty paid to the author for each sale rises with the cover price to a maximum. At the time of this writing, you earn about 35% of the cover price if your book is priced above a certain amount. Unless you are offering a loss-leader sale for promotional purposes, you want to price your ebook so that you earn the maximum royalty per sale. Same thing with your print book sales. Find out what your minimum price must be and set your cover price or the sale price accordingly.

Are you feeling overwhelmed yet? Yes, the promotional side of the writing coin can be pretty daunting to contemplate. You're learning a lot of new things, give yourself time to assimilate those new things. It's the lack of knowledge about 'how' to publish effectively that leaves writers with few sales and a lingering sense of failure. Well, hey, writing the book was a big task and you tackled that one scene or one chapter at a time, didn't you? You tackle promotion the same way. You take the promotional tasks one at a time. You're not going to 'fail' of you don't get everything set up and accomplished in a week, for heaven's sake! The worst that will happen is that your sales will be pretty flat until you get your promotional feet under you and start bringing your book to the attention of new readers. But unless you've decided to quit the day job right off (and I hope you have better sense than that), you can live with those flat sales while you get your promotional feet under you.

You are going to spend time. And you need to write, too. And you have a Life Outside of Writing.

Let's talk about these tough realities, shall we?

CHAPTER 8

Doing It!

No time is the aspiring writer's first excuse. I don't have time to finish the revision. I don't have time to start the next book. I don't have time for social media. I don't have time for blogging.

That's fine. We covered this, remember? Way back at the start of this book? If you don't have time, write when you do have time and when you finally get everything the way you want it, find someone to publish it or pay to publish it, and be happy with what you've done. There's nothing wrong with that. That bucket list 'I published a book' is a perfectly good personal goal. But do not expect that the book will magically take off and earn you a nice comfy retirement income. The chances of that happening are incredibly slim. At best. Buy the lottery ticket instead.

If your goal is to eventually make writing your main income or at least a strong secondary income, then you simply have to find the time. And it's there in your life, I guarantee you. Hey, I was a single mom with two young kids, family, friends, and a large country acreage with livestock when I set off to support the three of us with my words. There was no 'spare time' in my life. Our lives fill up with activities that quickly become habits and begin to feel 'necessary'. Habits are hard to break. (Remember this. It's important.) 'Necessary' isn't always so necessary. We stop after work at the local watering hole with friends or co-workers. We volunteer. We take fun classes or hit the gym every day. We jog or train for a marathon. The kids have soccer practice or other afterschool activities. You coach the team. There's housework. Yard work. Work your boss expects you to do at home. And of course, in the evening, there are movies, TV, that personal Facebook page with all those friends you need to keep track of. Lots of things to do and wow! There is simply no free time left.

Yes, that is a reality.

So what do you do?

First of all, let's look at your mindset. What I see very often, especially among aspiring women writers, is a sense that this is a hobby until proven otherwise, it's self-indulgent, and thus, it must come after every other little family/friend obligation on the schedule. You know what that means? Yep. You got it. You're never going to have writing time. You will not give yourself permission to put that writing ahead of anything. I have quite a few students like that, they're always late with an assignment, and they all have the same range of excuses; family, work, friends in need... They know better than to tell me that they didn't get it done because their TV schedule was too full or that the Facebook page takes 2 hours every night.

Be honest with yourself. Have you given yourself permission to pursue this as a new business, putting other things aside in the interests of that future income? Or do you really, deep down inside, feel that you can't put your writing first until you prove yourself by succeeding, by selling well and making money? Be honest, now! Your future success depends on that honesty. This 'I must prove myself' mindset is a deadly Catch 22. You will not succeed as a career author if you cannot devote the time to writing and promoting as if you are a career writer. You cannot get there by using the scant spare time left over from the activities that fill your life today.

Cannot.

Discouraged yet? Don't be. If you want the career, you can make that writing time happen. Yes, you really can. As I said, it's already there in your day. You're simply going to have to make some 'tough love' decisions.

Write this down on one of those sticky notes and put it up on the monitor (gee, it's getting a bit crowded up there, isn't it?). IT'S A DAY JOB Repeat after me; It's a day job. It's a day job. It's a day job. Would you tell your boss that you can't come in today because you have to watch that new episode of Whatever, or that your neighbor wants you to come out to the plant sale and have lunch after? If you do, you're probably not going to work there very long, are you? IT'S A DAY JOB. When I started out as a writer, every spare second went into my writing, and everything except my kids came after the writing on my priority list. I wasn't supporting us yet. I was scrabbling to find any writing job and any market that paid any money at all, and I was writing for those markets. We were dirt poor. There was no guarantee that I would ever 'make it'. I was boss and employee both, and believe me, I was a pretty tough boss. I had to be.

Yes, if you are supporting yourself and/or a family on your day job, you cannot quit it. You do have to pay the bills. But you can make writing your absolute number three priority, right after immediate family and pay-the-bills day job.

Putting It First

It means giving stuff up. It means negotiating with family.

What do you give up? How about TV, movies, stopping at that watering hole every night, keeping up with that huge list of Facebook friends, spending an hour at the gym every day, going out to dinner four times a week... Keep a week long diary. Begin right now. Continue on through bedtime, a week from now. List every activity that you do from the time the alarm goes off or you roll out of bed to the time you fall back into bed. Be honest. If you're sitting in front of that TV for two hours every night, put it down and name the shows, if they're regular favorites. Shopping, reading, yard work, visit with friends; write it all down.

Got it done? Okay, let's take a look at it. We're going to prioritize. We'll start with what you have to put first. That would be the necessary kid-time and the day job. If your kids are young and can't get themselves off to school without your physical assistance, you need to participate. But if they are old enough to get breakfast on their own and get themselves to the bus, let them do it. Teach them to do it. Require them to do it. You have a new day job and the boss will not tolerate tardiness! They'll grow up to become nice, self-sufficient kids who can cook for themselves, clean their rooms, and do their own laundry. That's a bonus. And you get that morning writing time. Do you really have to cook breakfast for your spouse? Can't he or she put a couple of pieces of toast in the toaster, fry an egg, or stick a frozen waffle in the microwave? Is that a gasp of horror I hear? Yeah, you are going to have to bring the family in on this career path, folks. You need to make this a family investment. This is a future income we're talking about here, remember? This is not just a self-indulgent hobby. This is for their benefit, too. You will have a job that allows you to be there for the family all the time rather than off at a day job elsewhere, and you'll bring in an income. They need to help you out. That's part of this 'career path' mindset. It is much more difficult to do if the family is not on your team. My sons learned to cook, wash clothes, and do basic housekeeping because I couldn't do all those things for them and still have writing time to pay the bills. They are now adults who have nice clean homes that they can keep clean themselves and are great cooks. Didn't hurt them a bit that they learned that stuff pretty young. Sure your family would rather you did that for them, ladies. But this is a new day job, and I bet they'd like the extra money from increasing book sales, huh?

It's a day job. It will benefit the family financially. It is not your self-indulgent personal hobby.

If you were taking a graduate course in order to qualify for a better paying job, you'd justify that study and class time to your family, wouldn't you? Writing is no different. Negotiate. When my kids were young and home a lot we'd make deals. Give me an hour to finish this chapter and we'll go to the park and play on the swings this afternoon. Watch a movie for an hour and let me work and we'll fill the wading pool when I get done. Kids are good at bargaining and they get it. You have to keep your end of that bargain and you have to be tough about them keeping their end of it. If you don't get that hour, they don't go to the park. You need to parent well, but this is a day job and they need to respect that.

Are your kids involved in tons of after-school activities and you have to drive them everywhere? Time to talk to other parents whose kids are in the same activities and make some carpooling arrangements. The price of gas makes it an attractive option to most parents. See if you can free up some time that way. Coming home tired from the day job with dinner to fix and homework to oversee? Delegate some of the work to the rest of the family. Remember...you're prepping for a job. You may not have the mental stamina to work for three hours every night, but plan on doing something on the book and the promotional platform, even if you merely make some notes for the next chapter or respond to a blog comment or two. If your evening seems packed with stuff you Must Do, go down that list and, one by one, ask yourself 'what will happen if I don't do this?'. If the answer is 'we have to call 911' do it. If the answer is merely socially embarrassing, don't do it. You'd be amazed at how flexible family members can be when they have to be. And you will survive the disapproval of friends or family who find your housekeeping lacking. Honest. Just stop inviting them over if it's too painful. When you start selling lots of books, hire a cleaning service. An author friend of mine, Diane, managed to avoid housework for years by writing and selling book after book. Nobody has died from visiting her home.

Now, let's look at your entertainment consumption. We have a finite number of 'free hours', when we're not engaged in the day job or family necessities. Think of that as your 'time dollar'. You can spend that time dollar many ways; on family, friends, TV or movies, eating out, clubs and entertainment, the after-work watering hole, gym, classes, volunteer work.... I'm sure you've included other activities as well.

Take a look at that list. Do you want a career or do you want to keep all your Facebook friends happy? Do you really care if they feel neglected? Do you really care if they unfriend you because you didn't reply to their endless chatter? Do you really have to know every trivial detail about everybody's life? And what about TV? Is that cop show really more important than a writing career? Or that sit-com? Or the reality show? If you were offered the good paying job of your dreams would you turn it down because you'd have to miss these shows in order to take it? Would you really?

Yes, it'll be hard! You're laboring away in front of that screen, all by yourself, you're not selling many books yet and all your friends are laughing and having a great time down at the restaurant or after-work watering hole. Or your family's enjoying themselves without you in front of the TV. You could be there having a great time, too! A writing career is not a source of instant gratification, that's for sure. That Viral Path is pretty darn narrow and steep at first and a lot of other things in life will make you feel much happier right now. It's hard to keep your eyes fixed on that distant goal of a self-sustaining career. It's hard to believe in it when you sold three copies of your first book last month. That's why so few authors persist and achieve that career for themselves. It's hard work and the pay is awful at first.

Do budget some fun time for yourself. Negotiation is part of this game, if you want to succeed long-term. If you really love that cop show or sit-com or reality show, make it a motivational reward. If I write one hour every day, next Wednesday I can take the evening off and watch my show. Or you can stop in at the bar with your friends after work. Or go out to eat. Whatever you really miss doing. Now you have a little reward for letting your chatty co-worker's call (that will cost you at least an hour of listening to her go on about her new boyfriend) go to voicemail, or putting up with a friend's rude kids in your carpool so that he'll take your kids to soccer practice on Tuesday nights. You put in those hours and on Wednesday, you sit down to your show or stop in at the bar, feeling that it's a well-earned reward for a writing-week well spent. Yeah, you'll miss those other shows you give up, but you know what? You'll get over it and pretty soon, you'll wonder why it seemed so hard to let go.

Yes, you're going to lose some controlling friends who just can't stand it that you don't come out and play when they want you to. Oh well. The really good friends will understand, maybe read your drafts for you, and comment. They will be thrilled that you are pursuing a life dream and willing to work so hard for it. Very few people have the guts to do that, and you'll get your share of admiration, don't worry. Maybe they'll even help you out – take your kids to the zoo to give you a weekend writing day or cover something at work for you. Treasure them. They are a treasure!

A spouse or life partner is wonderful, if he or she supports you. In all honesty, it will be very very difficult if not impossible to succeed with a writing career if your life partner is not supportive. Here again, you're going to need to negotiate. You fix your own breakfast in the mornings and I'll quit working at 9 to watch TV with you before bed. Planning a regular 'date night' is not a bad idea. Your partner is going to get a lot less attention from you if you're focused on that computer screen after work, so you need to make sure you both have time to play together. I can't say often enough that this career path needs to be a family matter. You cannot shut out the family and pursue the viral path on your own. They need to be on your side and, hopefully, helping you out.

Negotiate! Remember – it's future income and a job you cannot get laid off from! In this day and age of frequent layoffs, that is a huge plus.

Habits are Habit Forming

Our creative brain can take some coaxing to fire up, when we first start out as writers. There's nothing more frustrating than sitting at your screen as the minutes of your precious writing hour tick away and staring blankly at the screen. There are two remedies to that issue. The first, and most important, is to realize that you don't need the ephemeral presence of Your Muse to write well. Nope. You sure don't. Oh, I was like that at first, waiting for that moment when the creative brain woke up and the words seemed to flow onto the pages on their own. What joy! But then, I became a pro. Now I had deadlines. I accepted story and article assignments. And as a new author, I would shoot myself in not just one foot but both feet if I started missing deadlines.

So I wrote. Sometimes the muse was with me and other times she was on vacation somewhere or just didn't feel like getting out of bed today, thank you! Without that lovely sense of energy. I dragged every word out of my brain kicking and screaming and slapped them down on the pages like ugly toads. I cringed at what I was producing. I was sure that I was destroying my budding career, but I had to make that deadline.

After the fact, when I went back to read those toady pieces of forced creation...

Oh my gosh.

Mostly, they were just as good as the stuff I'd written in the throes of creative ecstasy. Really. Even without Lady Muse's pixie dust. Wow. What a revelation. In fact, one such 'forced' novella brought me to the exalted status of Hugo Award Finalist and won the Readers' Choice Award from Asimov's Magazine that year. The Hugo is the top award for fiction in the Science Fiction universe. Writing that story had been such a slog! And....it was good.

As I said. What a revelation. And it's not just me, folks. I get student apologies all the time; *'this is awful, I couldn't get into this piece, but I had to get it in on time...'* You know what? They're as good as the stuff the student usually sends in and more often than not, they're an improvement on the previous assignment. Your ability with words does not go away just because you don't feel creatively 'hot' today or you lack motivation. That's all in your head. If you wait for your muse to give you permission to write, good luck! Those muses are fickle critters! Nope, when that writing hour clock starts ticking, you start working. Revise the last scene to get yourself warmed up and then move into the next scene. So what if it seems awful to you now? Remind yourself that it's all in your head and you can delete it during the revision process if it really is bad. Do not delete it now. Keep working. You can fix everything in revision. If you're writing a post for your blog and don't feel inspired, too bad. Make it a writing exercise. Decide that you are going to entertain your readers by doing this particular piece. Now do this well. Work on voice, don't expect that glow of inspiration. Save it to review and post tomorrow. You'll probably find that it needs only minor tweaking.

Find a way to fit regular writing time into your life. Make it happen. If you write for a half hour during your office lunch hour or you skip that evening TV or Facebook time to write for an hour, you create a habit. You are going to sit down and write at this time every day. It doesn't take long before your creative brain starts waking up and getting into gear ahead of time, so that when you sit down to that regular writing hour or half hour, or fifteen minutes, it's ready to go. Won't happen every time, but just as your stomach starts rumbling a half hour before dinner time, your creative juices will usually start flowing as that writing time rolls around. It also helps with family and friends. If everybody knows that you're busy writing every evening from 8 PM until 9 PM and either don't answer the phone or are a bit testy, they'll stop calling you during that time. The kids, the spouse, will be comfortable with your absence and get used to taking care of their needs on their own for that period. You'll find that pretty soon, you are way more productive during that writing time than you were when you first began.

Time Sheets And The Tax Man

Let's start right out with the obligatory disclaimer here; I am not a tax professional (doing my own taxes makes me break out in hives and I love my CPA) and I am not giving any 'how to' advice in terms of what the IRS (or your national equivalent if you don't live in the USA) will or will not accept in terms of your tax preparation. But I have filed as a writer for many years now, which means that the IRS is satisfied that I earn my living primarily as a writer. It is a legitimate business, it is not a hobby. Because of that, I can deduct my expenses; paper, toner, purchases of books, computers, printers, and the like, travel expenses for writing projects or workshops, along with meals and lodging costs, dues and subscriptions to professional organizations and journals, and so on. These are the same types of expenses any business owner can deduct. You do need to consult a tax professional who is familiar with this type of deduction, especially if you work at home full time as I do, have a dedicated home office, and want to claim part of your utilities, mortgage, and so on as office expenses. The IRS has very stringent rules on what does and does not a home office make! (No, the guest room will not work for you).

The IRS does not require you to make money every year in order to file as a business. It does require you to conduct yourself as if you are a serious business rather than a hobbyist, if you are not yet making money. What does that mean? It means they want proof that you are making a good faith effort to become a self-supporting author. Proof you say? How do you supply proof without sales? Isn't this another Catch 22?

Nope. You use time sheets.

I still use a time sheet every single day. On it, I keep track of the time I spent during the day working on various client manuscripts, the time I spent on student work, the time I put into writing this book, writing stories or articles, working on the blog, on my newsletter, even answering emails. If the IRS has any question about whether I'm a business or a hobby, that auditor merely has to look at my time sheets. Yes, I'm devoting regular time daily to pursuing my business goals, I'm tracking my production and expenses, I am operating as a business.

I keep track of mileage as I take manuscripts to the post office or drive to conferences or workshops. If I fly somewhere to research an article for a magazine or attend a conference, I keep all my receipts for meals and hotel as well a record of my flight expenses. I do have a home office that could not conceivably be used for any other purpose and so I can deduct a percentage of my utilities and maintenance costs for the year.

Time sheets are your friend. As you struggle with your time budget to balance writing and promotional demands, the time sheet is a great way to track your actual time spent during the day. It's a way for you to get a sense of your own productivity, the ebb and flow of your writing time during the week. That will help you estimate how much time it might take you to, say, complete a writing project or have that book ready for publication. You can download and install a simple time tracking device on your computer or phone. Quite a few exist and many are free. I use one called Toggl that allows me to click a button when I start a project and click when I end it, to produce a record of the time spent. At the end of the day, those records of time spent go on the time sheet for the day. Looking at my time sheet for yesterday, I entered time spent answering business email, working on this book, client work, student assignments, and blog time for a total of 8.5 hours. I traveled to address a group in the evening, spending 2.5 more hours of my time, and I entered the 40 plus miles traveled in my mileage diary in the car, specifying which group I addressed. At the end of the month, I have a snapshot of my productivity and time spent. I can compare this month with other months to get a clear picture of how I am spending my time.

Even if you're depending on the current day job and can't claim that you're primarily a writer to the Tax Man, those time sheets are a great way to demonstrate to yourself that you are serious and a great way to get a clear sense of just where that time goes every week. I highly recommend them as a powerful tool to help you succeed.

Life Support

Support is crucial for your success. Writing is a lonely job and when you're starting out, it is so difficult to look ahead and really believe in that success you plan to achieve. It's very easy to get discouraged, very easy to feel that you're lousy, that nobody wants to read what you write. You need other writers, you need people who will cheer you on, read what you write, give you feedback as readers and/or writers. It is very difficult to keep up that grueling pace of career-building on your own. Writing has never been an instant-gratification business. Your readers may rave about you, but if they do that raving in Cleveland or Sweetwater, Texas, and don't bother to send you a fan letter, you don't know about it. It can feel as if you're dropping your words into a huge, echoing well.

Make some writer and/or reader friends if you're not already part of a live, local writers group. The internet makes this doable. Surf around a bit and find websites where writers and readers hang out. Check the bulletin board at local bookstores and libraries and see if any writers groups meet in your neighborhood. Online and in person writers groups can be a valuable resource. If your spouse is not all that interested in this writing stuff and your kids are busy with school, you really do need to find other people who will understand your frustration with the plot that has hit a dead end or the character who suddenly refuses to cooperate. Informed feedback from someone who can tell you 'I thought his motivation to help was kind of weak in chapter four' rather than, 'oh, it's great, honey!' is very valuable (even if 'oh it's great, honey!' feels so much better).

Do be a wary consumer, though. Writers groups need to click. If you join a group and are made to feel like a know-nothing amateur by the snooty 'regulars', high-tail it out of there! If you leave a group get-together every time feeling less confident and happy as a writer than you did when you arrived, this is not the group for you. Criticism can be thorough without being brutal, and you can hear about a lot of problems in your story while still feeling supported by the group. If the group seems to focus on 'what is wrong' rather than 'how to make it better', leave! Now! Run, don't walk! However, a group that constantly tells you that your story is wonderful, perfect, don't do a thing, is not helping you, either. You are writing for tough minded editors not your delighted-by-anything-you-do writers group. When a group no longer can give me useful criticism, I leave it. Nobody is perfect and I need someone who can spot the weaknesses.

If you can't find a group to join, find those writer boards, websites, or blogs to hang out on and make some connections with three or four other writers. Exchange manuscripts with them and see if you can't come up with some good writing buddies that way. Again, if the person you are exchanging with is not helping you, if all his or her comments are simply negative remarks about your comma usage, for example, or something equally trivial, excuse yourself from the relationship politely; *'gee, I'm just not going to have enough time to do this for awhile ...''* You're *not* going to have enough time, you're not lying. That time has to go to working with someone who is helping you grow.

Don't try to go this alone. It is indeed a lonely road and in the solo silence you'll hear the croaking of those shoulder vultures as they alight on the back of your chair; *You're no good, you're never going to make it, nobody wants to read what you've written....* A good circle of writer friends -- people who can point out the weak spots in your work but believe that you are going to succeed – is the best anti-shoulder-vulture defense out there! You're all on the same path, sharing the same hardships, the long slog, the discouraging early sales. You need each other

CHAPTER 9

Go Forth And Publish

Well, we've pretty well covered the topic, at this point. You should have a good idea of what 'self-publishing' or 'Indie publishing' means today, and more importantly, you should have an idea of whether or not this is how you want to proceed. By all means, try the big Legacy publishers first if your book suits their rapidly-narrowing market needs. Use what you've learned here to keep yourself safe from the sharks that want to scam you and see if you can't place the book there. It's very very difficult to pull off as a new writer, today, but if your book does end up on the New Releases shelf in the bookstore, you get a lot of attention right away and you can get a nice jumpstart on a fan base.

Just don't let those agent rejections make you feel like a failure. Remember that the Legacy houses are not interested in a 'good book', they are interested in a 'good book that sells a million copies'. Your book might be *good*, but have a more limited market. That 'more limited market', while not enough for New York, can still bring you a nice income eventually.

If the New York market isn't open for you, then make that decision; do you want to start building that business, spend the time and creative energy to pursue a career on your own? If the answer is no, there's nothing wrong with that. Use the consumer savvy you've learned here to find the right small commercial publisher for your book and let that publisher do the heavy lifting. Do as much or as little promotion as you have time and inclination to do and be happy with the fact that people are reading your book! You *are* a published author!

If yes, you decide that you want the day job, the career as a writer, the income that pays your bills, then have at it! It's hard work, you'll be discouraged at times, but you *can* do it. I did it. Keep your eyes on that goal, review those sticky notes you've stuck all over your monitor, and stay focused on that long tail. You'll get there. It won't be tomorrow, but you'll make it happen.

You know what?

It's a *great* day job.

Good luck, and write well, however you go forward!

Mary Rosenblum
The Literary Midwife
New Writers Interface
http://www.newwritersinterface.com

ABOUT THE AUTHOR

Mary Rosenblum attended the prestigious Clarion West Writers workshop in 1988, where she sold her first SF story to Asimov's Magazine editor Gardner Dozois and her writing career took off. She published multiple novels with NY publishers as Mary Rosenblum in SF and Mary Freeman in mystery, was a Hugo and Nebula finalist, won the Sideways and Compton Cook awards, and received a lot of critical acclaim for her fiction, both short stories and novels. She began teaching writing fifteen years and also works one-on-one with novice writers as a 'literary midwife' taking authors through drafts, final editing, publisher-matching, and self promotion of their books, to make sure it gets done well. She has twice returned to teach the Clarion West Writers workshop and lives in rural western Oregon where she flies a small plane to as many cool and faraway places as she can.